A WHOLESOME EXAMPLE

SEXUAL MORALITY
AND
THE EPISCOPAL CHURCH

A WHOLESOME EXAMPLE

SEXUAL MORALITY
AND
THE EPISCOPAL CHURCH

Robert W. Prichard

Editor

**BRISTOL
BOOKS**

A WHOLESOME EXAMPLE
Sexual Morality and the Episcopal Church
Copyright ©1992 by Robert W. Prichard

First Edition, May 1993

Chapter 7, "Homosexuality: The Behavioral Sciences and the Church," is re-printed with permission from Dr. William F. Hunter of the *Journal of Psychology and Theology*. The editorial offices of the journal are located at 13800 Biola Lane, La Mirada, California 90639.

Unless otherwise indicated, all Scripture quotations are from the *Revised Standard Bible* © 1946, 1952, 1971,1973 by the Division of Christian Education of the National Council of the Church of Christ in the U.S.A. Used by permission.

Scripture quotations indicated (NRSV) are from the *New Revised Standard Version Bible* © 1989 by the Division of Christian Educaion of the National Council of the Churches of Christ in the U.S.A. Used by permission.

ISBN 0-917851-71-4

Printed in the United States of America

BRISTOL BOOKS
An imprint of Bristol House, Ltd.
2201 Regency Road, Suite 301 • Lexington, KY 40503
Phone: (606) 276-4583
Fax: (606) 276-5365

To order, call our toll-free line: 1-800-451-READ

CONTENTS

ACKNOWLEDGMENTS

I wish to thank the many people who have provided support and assistance on this project. In particular, I thank Rae Dahlinger for her transcription of chapter 2, Nancy Brown for the extensive secretarial work that made this project possible, David Scott and Mary Hays for valuable editorial advice, Rev. Todd Wetzel of Episcopalians United for his considerable encouragement, and James Robb of Bristol House for his patient and constructive assistance.

In addition, I wish to thank Episcopalians United for their generous financial support of this project.

Robert W. Prichard
Alexandria, Virginia
March 1993

CONTRIBUTORS

Jennifer Lynn Craycraft is an undergraduate student at Eastern College in Pennsylvania. An active Episcopal lay person, she has written and spoken on matters of Christian sexuality. Forward Movement published her pamphlet entitled *Sense and Nonsense about Sex or No Sex.* She also spoke to two of the open hearings at the Episcopal Church's 1991 General Convention.

The Rev. Mary M. Hays is an Assistant Professor of Pastoral Theology and an Assistant Dean at Trinity Episcopal School for Ministry in Ambridge, Pennsylvania.

Stanton L. Jones, Ph.D. is an Associate Professor and the Chairman of the Department of Psychology at Wheaton College in Wheaton, Illinois. An Episcopalian, he is a member of the Diocese of Chicago's Commission on Human Sexuality. He has contributed to the discussion of human sexuality in the Methodist and Presbyterian Churches, and has written for *Christianity Today* and the *Journal of Psychology and Theology.* The article reprinted in this collection was co-written with Donald E. Workman, who in 1989 was a doctoral student in psychology at the Illinois Institute of Technology in Chicago.

The Rev. Judith M. McDaniel is an Assistant Professor of Homiletics at the Virginia Theological Seminary.

The Rev. Murray L. Newman, Th.D., is the Catherine N. McBurney Professor of Old Testament, Language, and Literature at Virginia Theological Seminary. He is the senior member of the faculty.

The Rev. Robert W. Prichard, Ph.D. is the Arthur Lee Kinsolving Associate Professor of Christianity in America at Virginia Theological Seminary. He is the author of *A History of the Episcopal Church*.

The Very Rev. Richard Reid, Th.D. is the Dean and President of Virginia Theological Seminary. He is also the Molly Laird Downs Professor of New Testament. Among his regular responsibilities is the teaching of courses on St. Paul's Epistle to the Romans.

The Rev. David Scott, Ph.D. is the William Meade Professor of Systematic Theology and Professor of Ethics at Virginia Theological Seminary. He served as vice-chair of General Convention's Commission on Human Affairs. He opposed the recommendations on same-sex unions and ordinations made by that commission to the 1991 convention.

The Rev. William S. Stafford, Ph.D. is the David J. Ely Professor of Church History at Virginia Theological Seminary. Among projects on which he is currently working is a book on the seven deadly sins.

The Rev. Elizabeth Zarelli Turner is the former Associate Rector for Christian Education of St. James' Episcopal Church in New York City. She has served as the editor of the *Ecumenical Bulletin* and was a contributor to *Men and Women: Sexual Ethics in Turbulent Times*.

The Rev. Joseph W. Trigg, Ph.D. is the Rector of St. Patrick's Church, Falls Church, Virginia and an Adjunct Professor at Virginia Theological Seminary. He is the author of *Origen: The Bible and Philosophy in the Third-century Church* and of *Biblical Interpretation*, volume 9 in *The Message of the Fathers*.

INTRODUCTION

In recent years the members of a number of American denominations—Episcopalians, Lutherans, Methodists, and Presbyterians, to name a few—have engaged in a rather spirited debate about sexual morality. While the specific terms of the debate have differed from one denomination to another, the debate as a whole has had a fairly uniform shape. It generally begins with some aspect of clerical morality: Should a certain behavior disqualify one from serving in the ordained ministry? (It is from this starting point with clerical morality that the title of this book is taken. In the Episcopal ordination office, candidates are asked whether they will pattern their lives and those of their households so that they "may be a wholesome example to all people.")

The attempt to define clerical morality leads to a broader discussion. Clearly, one cannot isolate one's judgment about moral behavior in clergy from one's judgment about moral behavior in the laity in the denominations they serve. The consideration of lay behavior leads, in turn, to a discussion of sexual values in the society at large. Since the 1960s, our society has been retreating from the claim that sexual relations belong exclusively in monogamous, heterosexual marriage and has been gradually accepting premarital, extramarital, nonexclusive and homosexual relationships. What begins as a debate on clerical behavior soon becomes a referendum over this new set of American sexual mores.

The acceptance or rejection of some or all of these mores as normative for the church has significant consequences. Acceptance of extramarital sex, for example, has important implications for one's understanding of biblical authority, for there are clear biblical prohibitions of adultery. The classification of a behavior as sin or grace-filled has consequences for one's doctrine of sin, and a church's decision that certain persons are fit or unfit to serve in the ordained ministry leads inevitably to a reexamination of the meaning of ordination. Finally, the very process by which denominations make decisions on these questions will effect the nature of future moral discourse.

The first edition of this work was prepared in the spring of 1991, as the Episcopal Church prepared for its 70th General Convention, which met in Phoenix in July of that year. The edition was printed privately and distributed in limited numbers to the bishops and deputies who attended the convention. In the months following the convention, however, the large number of requests for the edition led to a second printing and, ultimately, to this second edition.

This second edition incorporates several changes made in response to suggestions from those who read the first. The collection has been expanded with the addition of three chapters. A guide has been provided for those who would like to use the collection with parish study groups. The essay on Clerical Morality and Moral Discourse has been expanded to include the results of the 1991 General Convention and the 1991 report of the House of Bishops of the English General Synod. In addition, a number of minor editorial changes have been made. The major premise of the collection remains the same, however: Immediate and uncritical acceptance of current American popular moral standards would be premature and unwise. There may well be ways in which the church's stance on issues of personal morality needs to be changed, but such alteration should come only after deep engagement with the Scriptures and the Christian tradition. We hope that this collection will contribute to that ongoing discussion.

CHAPTER

1

Being Nineteen

Being nineteen isn't easy. Being a Christian nineteen-year-old is a little more tricky. Being a Christian, single, virgin, nineteen-year-old female can seem downright impossible. High school was lots of fun to survive: On the one hand, I had friends telling me how great sex felt, how much fun it was, and how it helped cement their relationships with their current significant others; on the other hand, I had friends with fatherless babies, friends with gonorrhea and herpes, friends who had had abortions, friends who had been date-raped, and friends with broken hearts. In my own life, both of the boyfriends I dated during high school had sexual relationships with others while they were dating me. According to an informal survey conducted in 1989 by my high school class of 686 students, I was one of only three to acknowledge being virgin at the time of graduation.

On Being Young and Single: A Challenge to the Church

Jennifer Lynn Craycraft

Things haven't changed much in college — even a Christian one. I still have friends who sleep around, friends who are pregnant, friends who have been raped and/or abused, friends with sexually transmitted diseases. They're the walking wounded, a representative sampling of the thousands of young adults and teenagers who succumb to the pressures surrounding us every day (or, in the case of rape and abuse, who suffer at the hands of someone else who has).

It's an easy mistake to make, really. The media certainly thinks that pre- and extramarital sex is acceptable. Adultery is glorified in movies like *The Woman in Red*. Even such wholesome television characters as "Doogie Howser, M.D." engage in premarital sex. Everything from breakfast cereal to cars to cigarettes is marketed using sex or sexual symbols, and magazines such as *G.Q.* and *Cosmopolitan* show us how to market ourselves. Many, if not most, of our friends are sexually active, not knowing what else to do in a relationship when things get a bit boring. Our bodies, moreover, are screaming at us to relieve the anxieties built up inside from hormones, stress, loneliness, and fears about the future.

> *In plain words, husband and wife are meant to be joined as virgins, and thereafter only to engage in sexual relations with each other.*

In the midst of all these mixed messages stand the biblical injunctions about holy sexuality and marital relationships. Whatever the world might be saying, God's view is that "Marriage should be honored by all, and the marriage bed kept pure" (Hebrews 13:4). In plain words, husband and wife are meant to be joined as virgins, and thereafter only to engage in sexual relations with each other. A hard teaching? Perhaps. Certainly a much healthier one than is typically being followed in a culture in which three out of five marriages end in divorce!

A typical romance these days runs along these lines: Boy and girl meet, are attracted to one another, and get to know one another (maybe). Shortly, they begin kissing. In an even shorter amount of time, they have sex. Then they begin to argue, to fight. Soon they part ways, both having lost a little more of themselves, and both desperately wanting to be made whole. Before long the scenario begins again. When (and if) they finally do get married, they find it extremely difficult to get beyond the playing of games and the telling of little lies to their partners. They never learned self-control or patience, so every time they have to wait for one of their desires—they call them "needs"— to be fulfilled, they feel cheated. Never having learned how to serve others, they hate the demands their spouses place on their persons and their time. Slowly, walls that were never quite torn down are rebuilt, and each begins to retreat inside a fortress of loneliness, self-pity, memory, and desire. In the end, each spouse sees the other as guilty of all the errors that threaten the relationship. It's all too easy to find someone else who is willing and lonely, too.

The fact is that premarital sex does not "cement the relationship." It rips it apart, turning whatever love and trust were present into a farce of unfulfilled promises. Sex makes us vulnerable to each other in a way that no other expression of love or affection can. Engaging in sexual relations before a deep and sincere trust, respect, love, and commitment have been developed is like eating cookie dough before it's baked. The batter may taste good initially, but it will eventually make the eater sick.

God designed guidelines for our sexual desires and marital relationships in order to help us experience the best marriages, and the best sex, possible. It is only through self-sacrifice and control, honesty, patience and prayer that a true love—the kind of love defined in 1 Corinthians 13—can develop. It is only with such a love that we can hope to experience happy, healthy marriages that live up to Jesus' "hard teaching" on the matter (Matthew 5:31-32; 19:3-12; Mark 10:2-12), and it is only in such marriages that we can enjoy sex as the beautiful expression of love and commitment that God created it to be.

Looking for Help

So where does a young, single person turn for help in following God's guidelines? To the media? Peers? A class on human sexuality? No, none of those sources seem to be helping very much. Well, then, how about the church?

I honestly wish I could wholeheartedly say yes to the last question, but, unfortunately, I cannot. Some churches seem to be having problems recognizing their teenagers and young adults as anything other than troublemakers, preferring to relegate them to the bottom of church life until they are married, raising a family, and bringing in a substantial tithe—if, that is, they stay around that long. Many other churches cannot even bring themselves to say "sex," let alone teach about it. Too many others have sold out to society's whims in an effort to be "modern" and relate to young people.

It's time for the church to start taking seriously its call to discipleship. As young women and men, we need people to speak God's truth to us in love, and then support us as we struggle to make that truth a reality in our lives. We need clerical and lay leaders who are able to talk about sexuality with the frankness of the Old Testament's Song of Solomon and yet have not forgotten the Christian call to holiness. We need to be in fellowship with people our own age who are facing the same daily pressures we face, so that we can encourage one another and hold one another accountable. We need to be in fellowship with the larger body also, so that we can learn from those who are older and more experienced, and so we can serve according to our capacities.

We need to have our spiritual gifts recognized, encouraged, and put to use. We need to have our singleness affirmed for the gift from God that it is, and we need to be able to talk to someone who will listen when we just don't feel like it's a gift. We are tired of attending "Singles' Ministries" that turn out to be dating services, and we're very tired of constantly hearing sermons on family life. How about doing a sermon series on singleness?

In short, we need the church to accept us as we are, challenge us to grow as men and women of God, and walk with us along the way. It won't be easy, and it won't always be fun. But then, neither is being young and single.

CHAPTER

2

Authority in Anglicanism

Anglicanism is a communion that takes authority—that which has legitimate command over people—very seriously. God is ultimate authority, but there are crucial mediate authorities.

The Bible and Sexual Ethics

Murray L. Newman and Richard Reid

Anglicanism has spoken of three such authorities in the church: the Bible, Tradition, and Reason. Recently, some Anglican scholars have suggested a fourth authority: Experience.[1] Whether three or four, these authorities do not stand on an equal footing (as in the old analogy of a three-legged stool) but in a dynamic hierarchy. The Bible is first and primary. Next, and lower, comes Tradition. Then follows human Reason, which is fallible and sinful. And finally, the most elusive and problematic authority (if it is included at all), Experience.

The Bible

Anglicanism has historically understood the Bible to consist of the 39 books of Hebrew Scriptures (the Christian Old Testament) and the 27 books of Greek Scriptures (the Christian New Testament). Anglicans have not considered the 15 or so intertestamental books recognized as canonical by the Roman Catholic and Eastern Orthodox communions as part of the Bible.

Tradition

Tradition includes the collective reflection of the church through the centuries on the biblical revelation, as well as new experiences in light of that revelation. For Episcopalians the core of the Tradition is the *Book of Common Prayer*, together with the *Hymnal 1982*.

Reason

Reason is the God-given human capacity (in the *imago dei*) rationally to observe, consider, categorize, and comprehend phenomena. The phenomena would include the Bible, Tradition, and all reality, natural and human. Human reason, of course, is both fallible and tainted by sin.

Experience

Experience probably should not be considered an official authority of the Church as such, but rather the field of play for the application of Scripture and Tradition, and involves contemporary perception (not exclusively rational) in natural and human reality of God's continuing and new, self-revealing activity. It is always to be tested by the common judgment of the community against the standards of Reason, Tradition and especially Holy Scripture.

The Nature of the Authority of the Bible

The Bible is the Word of God in the words of the faithful people of God and (as all Episcopal clergy declare when they are ordained) contains all things necessary for us and our salvation.[2] For the church, therefore, the Bible is the first and primary authority regarding the nature and activity of God, the nature of humanity, and God's will for humanity and the world.

The focus and center of Holy Scripture is the stream of history that began with Abraham and Sarah, and flowed through the times of Moses, Miriam, David, the prophets, the psalmists, the teachers of wisdom, to the exile, and beyond, to reach its climax in Jesus of Nazareth. In Jesus this historical stream revealed how God, the Creator of all things, uniquely demonstrated his presence, power, and purpose in a world of rebellious and sinful people.

Jesus Christ, in his life, teaching, death, and resurrection, is the perfect revelation of God, and the norm and touchstone of all else in the Bible. In the Bible, God reveals himself as personal, holy, righteous and loving. He is concerned to save people from all political bondage, as well as from the deeper bondages of sin and death. He is also willing to guide their lives as his special people of the covenant.

The life of the church represents a continuation of the biblical history. The Bible, which the church produced under God, is indispensable for the church's life, worship, discipline, theology, and ethics.

Under the guidance of the Holy Spirit, the church through its leadership—theologians, scholars, clergy, bishops, laity—has the responsibility and authority to interpret Holy Scripture, but every interpretation is ultimately subject to reevaluation in the light of new study of Scripture.

> *Christians pray that, by the power of the Holy Spirit, their hearts, minds and lives may be grasped and guided by his reality.*

The infallible norm and authority for the Christian church is God's revelation in Jesus Christ witnessed to in the Holy Scripture. This norm and authority, however, is never fully or perfectly grasped by the church in this world.

Christians pray that, by the power of the Holy Spirit, their hearts, minds and lives may be grasped and guided by his reality.

> Blessed Lord, who has caused all Holy Scriptures to be written for our learning: Grant us to hear them, read, mark, learn, and inwardly digest them; that, by the power of your Holy Word and guidance of your Holy Spirit, we may embrace, ever hold fast and faithfully proclaim the hope of everlasting life you have given us in our Savior Jesus Christ; who lives and reigns with you and the Holy Spirit, one God, for ever and ever. Amen.

The Scriptures are the primary authority for the church. By hearing, reading, marking, learning, and inwardly digesting them, Christians hold fast to the hope of everlasting life given by God in Jesus Christ.

The Old Testament and Sexual Ethics

The Pentateuch (The Torah, the Law) was the first section of the Old Testament to be canonized (about 400 B.C.). Consisting of the books of Genesis, Exodus, Leviticus, Numbers, and Deuteronomy, the Pentateuch is foundational and sets the tone and direction for the other two Old Testament sections, the Prophets and the Writings.

The first two chapters of Genesis make it abundantly clear that heterosexual marriage is the norm for the sexual activity of human beings. In the Genesis 2 account, Adam and Eve are created as helpers and partners for one another. Out of this union come children (4:1-2). The later priestly writing from about 450 B.C. articulates the essence of this male-female relationship:

> So God created humankind in his image, in the image of God he created them; male and female he created them. God blessed them, and God said to them, "Be fruitful and multiply . . ." (Genesis 1:27-28, NRSV).

In the earlier history of Israel (in the times of the ancestors and early monarchs) polygamy was practiced, but in the later periods it was superseded by strict monogamy (as witnessed by the book of Hosea and then the New Testament).

The exodus of the Hebrew slaves from bondage in Egypt is the determinative event of the Old Testament history. The response to the exodus event was the establishing of the covenant at Mt. Sinai, where the Hebrew people entered into a special relation with God and received the commandments to guide their life under him.

The divine commandments associated with Sinai are found in Exodus, Leviticus, Numbers, and Deuteronomy. They come from many different periods of the life of Israel and were formulated to express the divine will as new occasions required. They consist of moral, ceremonial, civil, and other types of regulations.

The first and basic commandments given in the covenant are found in Exodus 20:1-17, the Decalogue or Ten Commandments.[3] *The Book of Common Prayer* includes the Decalogue as an option in the Penitential Order:

> Hear the commandments of God to his people: I am the Lord your God who brought you out of bondage. You shall have no other gods but me.

You shall not make for yourself any idol.

You shall not invoke with malice the Name of the Lord your God.

Remember the Sabbath Day and keep it holy.

Honor your father and your mother.

You shall not commit murder.

You shall not commit adultery.

You shall not steal.

You shall not be a false witness.

You shall not covet anything that belongs to your neighbor.[4]

The Decalogue sets basic elements of personal morality—a rejection of the dishonoring of parents, murder, marital infidelity, theft, perjury, and covetousness—at the heart of what it means to be a covenant people, faithful to God.

Anglicanism has consistently held (with St. Paul, as in Romans 13:8-10, for example) that the moral commandments of the Old Testament (but not the ceremonial, civil, or other commandments) continue to be valid for the Christian.

In regard to sexual ethics, apart from the Decalogue, the unacceptable deviations from the norm of heterosexual marriage are particularly clear in Leviticus 18 and 20. These unacceptable sexual practices are:

a. *Incest* (18:6-18; 20:11-12)

b. *Adultery* (18:20; 20:10, 17, 19-20). Adultery is particularly serious, since it violates the marriage relationship.

c. *Homosexual relations* (18:22; 20:13). The plain sense of the story in Genesis 19 also clearly indicates a condemnation of the homosexual practices of the men of Sodom. Although their activity is not exactly hospitable, the effort of some to interpret the sin of these men as simple inhospitality strains credibility.

d. *Bestiality* (18:23; 20:15-16).[5]

The unacceptable deviations in Leviticus 18 and 20 are not unacceptable simply because they are Canaanite practices, as some have alleged. They would certainly have been no more acceptable if practiced in the name of Yahweh than if practiced in the name of Baal. New Testament authors, for whom the religious practices of the Canaanites were no longer a pressing concern, continued to find the deviations unacceptable.[6]

It matters greatly to the church what the Bible says about sexual ethics or indeed any other subject. The Bible has a preeminent authority. It is true that Anglicans interpret the Bible in the light of tradition and with the aid of reason guided by the Holy Spirit. But the Bible is clearly the first and primary authority, as the ordination vow that all Episcopal clergy take makes clear.

The New Testament and Sexual Ethics

As indicated above, it is important to understand the Bible as a whole and not simply to look at "proof-texts." The wider context of the Bible is important, and any discussion of sexual ethics in the New Testament must include reference to the Old. It is in that light that particular texts should be studied and considered. Nonetheless, particular texts do clearly contribute to the meaning of the whole and must not be neglected.

The context for understanding the New Testament position on homosexual behavior, then, must be the New Testament view on sexual behavior in general. Stated quite simply, the New Testament recognizes only two forms of sexual behavior as appropriate for Christians:

1. *Monogamous heterosexual marriage.* Such marriage is in principle lifelong and indissoluble, although St. Paul recognizes certain limited conditions under which a marriage may be dissolved and Matthew 19:3-9 includes Jesus' teaching that marital unfaithfulness is the one acceptable reason for divorce.

2. *Celibacy.* Jesus himself is the model of this behavior and St. Paul an example.

Clearly the norm for the vast majority is marriage. No form of sexual behavior other than these two is permitted.

Jesus explained that the basis for marriage is God's intention in creation itself: "But from the beginning of creation, God made them male and female. For this reason a man shall leave his father and mother and be joined to his wife, and the two shall become one" (Mark 10:6-8, RSV). Marriage then is part of the order of creation. As such it is accepted throughout the New Testament. Jesus states with apparent approval in Luke 20:34 that the people of this age marry and are given in marriage. He offers no apparent opposition to this even though in the Kingdom of God there will be no marriage.

Paul clearly approves of marriage although he is somewhat reluctant for people to take on that responsibility in light of the nearness of the end of the world. He prefers the other New Testament option of celibacy. In an important passage, however, he notes that those who cannot remain celibate should marry. He says, ". . . it is better to marry than to burn with passion" (1 Corinthians 7:9). Clearly for Paul marriage is a concession, the only alternative to celibacy. No other possibility is offered.

Hebrews 13:4, too, clearly affirms marriage: "Marriage should be honored by all, and the marriage bed kept pure, for God will judge the adulterer and all the sexually immoral."

> *Paul clearly approves of marriage although he is somewhat reluctant for people to take on that responsibility in light of the nearness of the end of the world.*

The New Testament affirmation of marriage leads to an opposite view on the appropriateness of other forms of sexual behavior. The passage just cited contains a key term, which the *Revised Standard Version* translates as "immoral." The word in Greek is *pornos*. A number of words are derived from this root, the most important being *porneia*.

The precise meaning of this word is difficult to establish. William Countryman argues that it means "harlotry" but recognizes that it has a wider meaning than "prostitution."[7] Clearly in Matthew 5:32 and 19:9 it means, or at least includes, adultery. In 1 Corinthians 5:1 it refers to incest. It is a word that covers a variety of sexual behaviors, all of which are regarded as outside Christian ethical norms. While there is no direct evidence that it explicitly refers to homosexual behavior, *porneia* seems to be a generic term for sexual activity outside of a proper marriage. It clearly includes adultery and incest. It may also include fornication and homosexuality.

Hauck and Schulz in their article on *porne* and related words in the *Theological Dictionary of the Bible* note that "the NT is characterized by an unconditional repudiation of all extra-marital and unnatural intercourse."[8]

Romans 1:26-27

This is clearly the key passage in the New Testament on the subject of homosexuality. Although some have tried to argue that the real issue here is idolatry, even many advocates of acceptance of homosexual activity now concede that Paul is speaking about homosexual behavior in this passage.[9] Paul argues that such behavior is wrong because it is "contrary to nature." That is a frequently used argument in both Jewish and Hellenistic literature.[10] For Paul it clearly is important.

> *Homosexual activity is one of many examples of a distortion of God's intention in creation.*

Despite general agreement about the reference to homosexual behavior here, some have argued that Paul does not actually mean to condemn that behavior. John Boswell, for example, argues in *Christianity, Social Tolerance and Homosexuality* that "the point of the passage is not to stigmatize sexual behavior."[11] This is quite true, but it does not alter the fact that Paul understands homosexual behavior as clearly morally wrong. Homosexual activity is one of many examples of a distortion of God's intention in creation.[12]

Boswell also argues that Paul refers here only to homosexual activity on the part of persons who are heterosexual.[13] He says "The whole point of Romans 1, in fact, is to stigmatize persons who have rejected their calling . . . . It would completely undermine the thrust of the argument if the persons in question were not 'naturally' inclined to the opposite sex . . . ." He then concludes that Paul would not have objected to homosexual behavior on the part of those who were "naturally" homosexual.

Boswell's assertion is clearly unfounded. Richard B. Hays's review of Boswell's argument states the issue very clearly:

> . . . to suggest that Paul intends to condemn homosexual
> acts only when they are committed by persons who are

constitutionally heterosexual is to introduce a distinction entirely foreign to Paul's thought-world and then to insist that the distinction is fundamental to Paul's position. It is, in short, a textbook case of "eisegesis," the fallacy of reading one's own agenda into a text.[14]

In other words, it is clear that Paul in Romans 1 does condemn homosexual behavior. He does this, as Hays also shows, because homosexual behavior is a distortion and violation of God's intention in creation.[15]

Other New Testament Passages

The other New Testament passages that seem to speak about homosexuality are in some dispute. 1 Corinthians 6:9, according to the *RSV*, lists homosexuals among those who will not inherit the kingdom of God. Two words appear in the Greek text at this point; the *RSV* translates both by the single word "homosexuals."

The first word is *malakoi*, which is a common word meaning soft. It is sometimes used in a metaphorical sense to mean "effeminate," and sometimes it also is used to describe young boys who were the objects of homosexual acts. The other word, *arsenokoitai*, appears for the first time here in 1 Corinthians. It comes from two Greek words meaning "male" and "bed" and may mean "those males who engage in homosexual acts." Both Boswell and Countryman suggest other meanings.[16] Certainty is not possible, but the most highly respected commentary on 1 Corinthians defends the intention of the *RSV* translation as the likely meaning.[17]

A recent observation by David F. Wright supports this reading. Wright noted the similarity between Paul's use of *arsenokoitai* and the Septuagint's text of the Holiness Code. (The Septuagint is the pre-Christian Greek version of the Jewish Scriptures which was adopted by Greek speaking Christians.) Wright concludes that the word *arsenokoitai* was formed "under the influence of the Septuagint texts of Leviticus 18:22 and 20:13," which explicitly condemn homosexual acts.[18]

The word *arsenokoitai* also occurs in 1 Timothy 1:10. The meaning there, however, is not certain.

To sum up, the fundamental fact is that the New Testament affirms heterosexual marriage as the only proper setting for sexual intercourse. That assertion derives primarily from the intention of God in creation itself. All other forms of sexual intercourse are wrong. Paul explicitly mentions homosexuality as one of the wrong forms. 1 Timothy, 2 Peter, and Jude may also do so.

The Contemporary Relevance of Biblical Texts

Some critics of the biblical view of sexual morality do not dispute the meaning of the passages on sexuality; rather they question whether biblical views on sexuality have any relevance for contemporary Christians. William Countryman, for example, argues that biblical norms about sexual ethics are based on purity codes and property codes. The purity codes no longer apply for Christians, and the property codes do so only if greatly modified. He draws the conclusion, therefore, that the sexual ethics of the New Testament are alien to the world of today.[19] He means not just that they are frequently not observed, but that they are irrelevant.

Countryman's dismissal of the purity codes as having any validity for modern Christian ethics seems to me to go entirely too far. The New Testament makes a clear distinction between the food laws which are abrogated for Christians and issues of sexual behavior. As Countryman himself recognizes, Paul makes the distinction very sharply in 1 Corinthians 6:13-20. Countryman also fails to take into account the importance of the creation story as a basis for the New Testament's view of sexual ethics. The New Testament constantly affirms the validity of the Old Testament's sexual ethical norms, which also are rooted in that creation story.

While this chapter intends to show that both the Old and New Testaments regard homosexual activity as sinful, that does not mean it is the only, or even the most serious, sin. The issue is whether the church can accept homosexual behavior as a "wholesome example" in accordance with the question asked all would-be Episcopal clergy during their ordination [see the *Introduction*, page 8]. The Scriptures clearly say no. Their unambiguous witness should warn the church not to bless any sexual activity outside of heterosexual, monogamous marriage.

CHAPTER

3

The Patristic period (roughly speaking the second through the fifth centuries) has traditionally had a special importance for Anglicans. The Reformers appealed to the writings of that period against what they took to be Romish perversions of the gospel. For later Anglicans the Fathers provided a congenial alternative to Romanism on the one hand and to Puritan Calvinism and biblicism on the other. From the seventeenth century to the present, Anglicanism has produced distinguished scholars of the Patristic period.

Human Sexuality and the Fathers of the Church

Joseph W. Trigg

The Fathers' teaching concerning human sexuality was not original. They reiterated the New Testament witness to the place of sexuality in God's plan and elaborated on some of its implications. They shared with the New Testament the sense that human life achieved its full purpose in obedience, not in self-actualization. Obedience in the sexual sphere took two forms: renouncing sexuality in celibacy or realizing sexuality in marriage. Gregory of Nazianzus referred to these two states as "the two divisions of life."[20] Augustine similarly referred to marriage and celibacy as the two good states of life.[21] There was no legitimate expression of sexuality outside these divinely given states of life; this was the basis for condemning adultery, homosexual behavior, and fornication.

Christian teachers made a point of rejecting the double standard prevailing in their society which condoned extramarital sexual activity on the part of men but did not tolerate it in women who were not prostitutes. Up until the fifth century it was normal for parents to postpone baptism of boys because it was assumed that they would, like Augustine, engage in premarital sexual activity, or, like Augustine's father, have extramarital sexual relations with concubines or prostitutes. By not being baptized young men avoided the church's penitential discipline.[22] Peter Brown's recent work, *The Body and Society: Men, Women, and Sexual Renunciation in Early Christianity*, points out that early Christianity made asceticism a positive and socially liberating alternative to marriage.[23]

> *[H]omosexual behavior was not a particularly important issue for the Fathers, but wherever it was mentioned it was condemned.*

Homosexuality, the principal area of human sexuality that the Episcopal Church is considering at this time, raises particularly difficult problems for those who look to Patristic sources for guidance, because we are dealing with writings from a culture that did not understand human sexuality as we do. One has only to read K. J. Dover's magisterial work *Greek Homosexuality* to see how very different homosexuality was within the ancient cultural context.[24] Any equivalent of the word "homosexual" or, for that matter, "heterosexual" does not occur in ancient languages, because the concept of sexual orientation toward persons of one's own or the other sex did not exist for them. William Peterson, in several recent articles, has argued cogently that, for this reason, the word "homosexual" should be avoided in translations of the Bible or the works of the Fathers. Nonetheless, while the Fathers were not aware of homosexuality in the way it is understood in the modern world, they were well aware of homosexual behavior, which was pervasive and socially acceptable in Greco-Roman society.

As in the case of the New Testament, homosexual behavior was not a particularly important issue for the Fathers, but wherever it was mentioned it was condemned. Arguably, there was relatively little mention of homosexuality in Patristic literature because there was no debate on the subject, it being understood that any sexual behavior outside of marriage was prohibited. The position recently argued by John Boswell—that homosexual relationships were acceptable in the church before the twelfth century—does not square with the Patristic sources. Peterson makes the caveat that "rejecting the translation 'homosexuals' does not mean that Christian tradition viewed same-sex sexual acts positively, for it did not."[25]

The Fathers rarely dwelt on homosexual behavior, but they did not hesitate to state their opposition to it. Christian writings, beginning with the *Didache*, one of the oldest outside the New Testament, regularly condemned *paidophthoria* ("corrupting boys") or *arsenokoitia* ("lying with males") along with adultery and fornication.[26] Interestingly, they did not rely on the Levitical prohibitions; neither Origen nor Theodoret, authors of the only Patristic commentaries on that book that survive, even referred to the prohibitions of homosexual behavior in Leviticus. Eusebius contented himself with pointing out the consistency between Leviticus and Plato in prohibiting such behavior.[27]

The Fathers clearly read the story of Sodom in Genesis 19 as implying the condemnation of homosexual behavior, which, like Paul, they consider "against nature." They began, at least by the fourth century, to refer to such practices as "sodomy."[28] A passage from the *Apostolic Constitutions*, a manual of church order compiled in Syria in the fourth century, provided a good summary of Patristic teaching on human sexuality, making clear the church's opposition to the ethical standards that prevailed in the larger society.

> For this reason, well beloved, flee such practices [adultery and fornication] because they are pagan [literally "Greek"] affairs. We do not react with loathing to the dead, as they do, because we hope that they will return again to lives, and we do not in any way bring legitimate unions into disrepute, even though it is their custom to profane such things. The union of a man and a woman, when it is legitimate, corresponds in fact to the will of God. Because

in the beginning he who created them male and female blessed them saying "Increase and multiply and fill the earth." If then the sexual differentiation exists by the will of God and to give birth to numerous offspring, it is clear that the union of man and woman also corresponds to his will, but this is not the case at all for the abominable union contrary to nature nor for unlawful acts that are hateful to God. For the sin of the Sodomites and bestiality are against nature, and adultery and fornication are unlawful; the one are acts of impiety and the other acts of injustice, both are, in the end, sins none of which will escape judgment, which each of them will obtain in proportion to its seriousness. For among these sinners, the first class provoke the dissolution of the world order, in permitting themselves to make use of nature in a way contrary to it, the second class, in the one case injure each other by destroying marriages and putting asunder the unity created by God, making children defiant and exposing the legitimate spouse to ridicule, in the other case fornication is the corruption of one's own flesh, since it is not intended for procreation but seeks only pleasure, which is a sign of intemperance and not at all a mark of virtue.[29]

In spite of the universality of such sentiments, John Boswell professes to find a positive attitude toward homosexuality in the Fathers' toleration of and participation in same-sex friendships. He believes that he can do this legitimately because, "from the scholar's point of view, any distinction between 'friendship' and 'love' must be extremely arbitrary." The two states, far from representing a fundamental dichotomy, "are simply different points on a scale measuring a constellation of psychological and physiological responses to other humans."[30] He goes on to state that "considering that even the individuals involved are often not absolutely certain whether their relationship is erotic or not, it is unrealistic to expect that ancient and medieval records will be able to offer some sure means of distinguishing between friends and lovers."[31] In effect, this means that evidence, or supposed evidence, of passionate same-sex friendships can be cited as evidence of homosexuality even if the actual cases cited gave no hint of genital, sexual activity. Thus it could be argued that a number of persons revered as saints from the Patristic period were actually homosexuals.

The cases Boswell cites are not convincing, even in his own terms. Boswell suggests that "the appeal of the love of two women" accounts for the popularity of the Martyrdom of *Perpetua and Felicitas*.[32] One might more easily attribute that appeal to Perpetua's deeply moving first-hand account of her trial and imprisonment, which forms the heart of the document, and to her pathos as a young mother at odds with her pagan family. If any explanation is needed for why Felicitas, alone of the four martyrs who died with Perpetua in 203, is named in the title with her, one does not need to look for any love interest. Felicitas is not depicted as having any special relationship with Perpetua. On the other hand, one could easily explain the focus on her by the pathos of her situation as a pregnant matron who gives birth in time to be martyred with the others and by the beauty of the two names together, appreciated by Augustine, who spoke of their winning "the prize of perpetual felicity."[33]

John Boswell professes to find a positive attitude toward homosexuality in the Fathers' toleration of and participation in same-sex friendships.

Boswell cites as another example of an erotic same-sex relationship Augustine's intensely emotional youthful friendship, vividly described in Book IV of his *Confessions*, with another young man. He states that Augustine "bitterly regretted the sexual aspect of such passions," citing, out of context, a passage about lust and desire from Book III.[34] In Book IV Augustine readily admitted to "uncleanness of such affections" (*talium affectionum immunditia*), but what made the relationship unclean was that it was not based on God's love shed abroad in the heart by the Holy Spirit. For Augustine, actual physical relationships, the power of which he also describes in compelling terms, were with female concubines. He cherished intimate friendships with other men throughout his life and was shocked by the notorious rupture of the once intimate friendship between Jerome and Rufinus.[35]

Boswell also stated that Paulinus, the Bishop of Nola venerated as a saint, "passionately loved" his elderly teacher Ausonius and gave expression to that love in "poetry of exquisite tenderness."[36] Paulinus was, indeed, a man of delicate sensibilities, but there is no more reason to think that his relationship with Ausonius was expressed physically than was his even more exquisitely tender relationship with Felix, the long-dead martyr whose shrine at Nola he administered as bishop, a relationship beautifully described in Peter Brown's *The Cult of the Saints*.[37]

What sort of conclusions can we draw from the witness of the Patristic period of issues confronting us today in relation to human sexuality in general and homosexuality in particular? First, we must acknowledge that the Fathers challenge our understanding of sexuality as primarily a means of self-actualization, just as they reject claims for human autonomy in other spheres. Conformity to God's will, not self-actualization, is primary for human relationships. Second, the Fathers did not hesitate to reject the prevailing mores of their society in light of the biblical witness as they understood it. Finally, the Patristic period is consistent with the witness of the Christian tradition in other times that homosexual behavior has no place in God's order for humanity. If, indeed, one defines any passionate relationship between persons of the same sex as "gay" or "lesbian" because of the supposed impossibility of distinguishing between friends and lovers, one can do so, but the existence of such supposedly gay and lesbian relationships among saints in the past cannot be used to bless physical unions between persons of the same sex in the present.

At the same time, we must be aware of the limitations of the Patristic witness. Peterson points out that the empirical research of modern social sciences, in developing the concept of sexual orientation, has "gained a better grasp of the ambiguities and complexities of human sexuality" than the Fathers possessed.[38] While it is utterly bogus to appeal to the Fathers in support of current efforts to alter the church's teaching on sexual behavior, we should be aware that they cannot provide any direct answers to our questions. An honest and constructive engagement with the Fathers, as part of a general attempt to come to terms with the Christian tradition on matters of human sexuality, has yet to happen. We cannot presuppose what the outcome of such an engagement would be. But if we are true to our heritage as Anglicans, we will not change our doctrine and practice in matters of human sexuality until such an engagement with the tradition has occurred.

CHAPTER

4

The sexual revolution of the last decades has not usually claimed Christian tradition as a friend. Some liberators (M. Daly, C. Heyward) see traditional sexual morality simply as an evil. Others (J. Fletcher, W. Countryman) consider it a very early mistake by Christians, the intrusion of Jewish legalism into the law of love. Until recently,

Sexual Norms in the Medieval Church

William S. Stafford

however, even the critics assumed that the prohibition of sexual intercourse outside of marriage had in fact been common tradition from the second century on. Recently, however, this assumption has been questioned. Some Episcopal and Roman Catholic

Christians, who wish their churches to be free of old "rigidities," also have enough respect for tradition to wish to find precedents in the Christian past for blessing the non-married sexual relationships they think right and proper now.

This attitude was clearly expressed in the resolution passed at the San Francisco convention of Integrity on July 3, 1989. It "calls upon the Standing Liturgical Commission of the Episcopal Church to prepare appropriate rites to restore to Lesbians and Gay men the ancient practice of sacramentally legitimizing our unions." The view seems to be spreading—it is a venerable myth, with its own long history—that the church was once far more tolerant of sexual activity than it later became. This chapter tests that view by examining the author's special period of study, the Latin middle ages.

Europe in the Eighth to the Fifteenth Centuries

Between the eighth and fifteenth centuries, the Western church embraced an astonishing variety of peoples, social structures, cultures, and conditions of life. From the cattle-raiding tribes of the *Scoti* in Ireland to the Byzantines in central Italy; from Germanic slaves working the soil to Provençal nobles professing delicate love poetry and equally delicate heresies; from agrarian hamlets to the houses of the great urban oligarchies: the middle ages included an enormous range of human life. As time passed, conditions changed radically. The poor, brutish, and short life-style produced by centuries of invasion prior to the tenth century gave way to the magnificence of Florence and Venice in the fourteenth century.

Within this social diversity, of course, sexual life took many forms. Among aristocrats, marriage might occur even in childhood; English peasants usually did not marry until their mid-twenties.[39] It was often accepted that men could have passionate friendships among men. There were many sorts of families, and many ways to live without a family. No doubt every possible sex act was attempted by someone at some time during this period.

Medieval pastors had to apply the tradition they had received from the ancient world to very different peoples . . .

Medieval pastors had a difficult job. They urgently needed to transmit the apostolic message of Christian faith and life accurately and faithfully. They were intensely concerned with continuity. This was not surprising, since any sort of continuity of life had been so hard to win from the warfare and social chaos of the early middle ages. Medieval pastors would transmit as best they could (usually in a highly condensed and edited form) what the Scriptures and Fathers had taught about sexual behavior. Yet many of their listeners were not like the people the

Fathers had known in the great cities of classical antiquity. Some were newly converted from pagan religions whose ethical values and sexual practices had little similarity to Christianity. Until late in the period, the new peoples were all peasants or military aristocrats, not urban merchants and workers. They were tribally organized, not individualistic. Steeped in the oral culture of their ancestors, they were not leavened by classical education. Medieval pastors had to apply the tradition they had received from the ancient world to very different peoples, in circumstances which were often quite new.

On one hand, the people had to be taught how to behave in ways that would not destroy the grace of their baptism. Yet various forms of sexual behavior that the Christian tradition considered wrong were deeply rooted in social structures. In Saxon society, for example, polygamy and concubinage were widespread and divorce easy; that flatly contradicted Jesus' own teaching. Abduction and forced marriage were common in Gaul. Troubadours made a virtue of adultery in Provence. Boys given to monasteries everywhere had to be dissuaded from having sex with each other, and consecrated virgins had to be protected from "seduction." The church had to confront and reshape sexual behavior that had deep social roots.

On the other hand, it was inevitable that the people's sexual mores would make themselves felt in the clergy's own sexual teaching. The clergy came from the people and had to deal with the people. So, for example, patterns of folk-marriage soon showed up in the missals: the old betrothal with hands and ring and gifts, but now at the church door in front of the priest; the boisterous marriage feast, but with the (celibate) priest finding himself sprinkling the marriage bed and the soon-to-be joined bodies with holy water before beating a hasty retreat.[40]

Fixed Points of Christian Moral Teaching

Amid this complex situation one may observe a few fixed points which every Christian teacher and pastor in the middle ages treated as certain. These fixed points were explained, rationalized, prayed, applied, enforced, and interpreted in quite different ways. They themselves, however, did not change. One finds them everywhere. First is praise for virginity and Christian celibacy. Second is acknowledgment of the lifelong marriage of a woman and a man as good. Third is a list of prohibited sexual acts. Such lists varied in their extent, but they may all be summarized as ruling that any sexual acts outside of marriage were wrong.[41]

Praise of Celibacy

It is not strange that the first fixed point—praise of Christian virginity, celibacy, and continence—was universal. Most medieval pastors were themselves supposed to be celibate; many of them freely chose continence. Celibacy was, after all, traditional. Jesus and his blessed Mother had both been virgins. The ascetic movement of the fourth century had transmuted the widows and celibates of early churches into a mighty river of renunciation, which flowed powerfully throughout the middle ages. Anchoresses like Julian of Norwich, scholars like Alcuin, noble women like Lady Margaret Beaufort, lovers like Francis of Assisi, soldiers like the Hospitalers, poets like Hildegaard took vows which consecrated them sexually to Christ alone. Every bishop had formulae to administer such vows. There can have been few corners of Europe where such people were not present. Memorials in speech, song, glass, and stone praising their action were to be found on every side.

Celibacy was, after all, traditional.

Celibacy was explained in many ways, of course, not all entirely consistent with each other: to embrace Christ directly; to give witness to the life of the resurrection; to set aside a distraction in contemplation or an impurity in going to the altar. The medieval church did not lack for witnesses to Jesus' word that marriage is not eternal.[42] Celibacy was a fixed point.

The Goodness of Heterosexual Marriage

Second, marriage between one man and one woman for life was acknowledged as good.[43] In spite of the great diversity of sexual arrangements among the new peoples, and in spite of the power of the ascetic current among Christians, the medieval church's validation of marriage held firm.

In some monasteries the acknowledgment was so reluctant and hedged with so many qualifications that it seemed very pale. In others, marriage was considered so divine that it became a formal object of contemplation.[44] But it had to be acknowledged as good, or else the inquisitors would come calling.

Clergy missals and manuals contained forms for blessing marriages. Scholastic theologians gave marriage extended treatment as a sacrament. The canon law wove jurisprudence through it. Its goodness was a fixed point.

Prohibited Acts

The third fixed point is a conventional list of prohibited sexual acts. One finds such lists either explicitly or implicitly included wherever sex was discussed by pastors. They are found, formally or informally, in rites of penance, conciliar legislation, sermons, liturgies, theological or canonical debates, and correspondence.

In such lists particular deeds were listed as wrong in themselves, like adultery, fornication, rape, incest, bestiality, and sodomy. The lists varied, of course, in how extensive they were. Yet they precluded sexual acts outside of marriage, and none of them suggested that any sexual act performed outside of marriage was in itself right.[45]

The Difficulty of Sexual Life

One might perhaps introduce a fourth constant, a bit less explicit than the others. The medieval church always expected that Christian sexual life would be difficult for almost everyone, whether celibate, married, or unmarried. No one, without the gift of quite extraordinary grace from God, could expect a life of unbroken sexual tranquillity.

One finds this expectation in the Leonine and Gelasian sacramentaries with their special masses against "temptation of the flesh" and "evil thoughts"; in the Celtic penitentials, with their detailed prescriptions for the penances to be performed by all sorts of people for all sorts of deeds; in the divorce legislation of the Decretals; and in theologians like Thomas Aquinas, who considered the temptation to fornication almost the most difficult of all, since it was so natural and so overwhelmingly pleasant.[46] After Adam and Eve were expelled from the Garden of Eden, anyone trying to follow God's plan for sexual life would find conflict. And yet anyone could find grace, too: repentance, forgiveness, and the mind and will to walk God's hard road.

I am not suggesting that there was a single, uniform sexual theology in the middle ages. There was not. The fixed points occur universally, but they were not explained or enforced in the same ways everywhere. Some marriage liturgies, for example, explained that God blessed marriage for the sake of procreation; others dwelt on the mutual joy and love of the man and woman becoming one flesh.[47] Some penitential manuals tried to regulate what went on in the marriage bed; most let it alone.[48] Thomas Aquinas explained that fornication is wrong because the sinners have not provided for the potential child, who would need both a father and mother to be reared adequately.[49] Some penitentials, however, treated fornication as a form of ritual uncleanness.[50] Peter Damian demanded that habitual homosexual acts debar one from ever serving as a priest; the pope to whom he wrote thought that penalty somewhat too severe if the offender repented.[51] In Ireland, married clergy came away from their wives and were reconciled to their bishops once a year and then went back to their wives.

> *The Christian tradition is a deep ocean, and many sorts of fish swim in it. Yet by the middle ages the shoreline was usually definite, even in times of flood or drought.*

These inconsistencies reflect the diversity of eight centuries of life among many peoples. The Christian tradition is a deep ocean, and many sorts of fish swim in it. Yet by the middle ages the shoreline was usually definite, even in times of flood or drought. Explanations and applications varied, but the fixed points did not.

Sexual Liturgies

The consistency of the church's teaching on the fixed points is plain in the sexual liturgies of the Latin church. Virtually all pontificals (liturgical books for bishops) contained forms for consecrating virgins or widows, for dedicating persons to religious seclusion, and otherwise admitting men and women to lives of vowed celibacy.[52] In most of them, the theological accent was on the love of Christ. The virgin longed for the immediate union with him which marriage signified. Other such liturgies emphasized the struggle to remain chaste. Yet all of these liturgies institutionalized the medieval church's praise of continence.

In medieval Latin service books, the liturgies for marriage differ from each other in many ways.[53] Most grounded marriage in God's blessing in Creation, which neither the Fall nor the Flood erased.[54] Many, although not all, drew the union of the woman and the man into a mass celebrating the Holy Trinity, in which the divine unity of Persons was the keynote of praise. Some orders (not all) reminded the marriage party of the superiority of celibacy by mentioning Jesus' virginity,[55] by excluding second marriages from parts of the marriage blessing,[56] or by exhorting the newly married couple to refrain from intercourse for three days. Yet those same service books required the priest to go bless the marriage bed. In spite of the many exceptions to any rule, on the following three matters the books are unanimous.

The Marriage of Man and Woman

First, every one of the liturgies I have examined baldly and unambiguously names the participants as a man and a woman. The words vary: *vir et mulier, famulus et ancilla, Monsieur et Madame, Jean et Marie, sponsus et sponsa.* The intention does not vary.[57]

My extended search among medieval service books and other sources for blessings of same-sex unions, alluded to in the Integrity resolution cited above, has turned up completely empty. In 1988 Professor John Boswell did claim to have discovered such liturgies, and his claim was widely reported in the church press. Four years have passed, however, and Boswell has yet to publish any evidence to buttress his claim. Invisible liturgies are difficult to evaluate, the more so since Boswell's reported claim is completely unparalleled and unsupported from other sources. If there is any such text, it must be published, so that its precise character and context is subject to scholarly analysis. Unless and until that is done, for other parties to cite "the ancient practice of sacramentally legitimizing" male gay and lesbian sexual unions amounts to disinformation.[58]

Marital Faithfulness

Second, the liturgies I have examined all make the woman and the man promise faithfulness and exclusivity. The *Ordo Leodiensi*, for example, puts the vows for the man this way:

I N.N. give the faith which I received in the sacred font to N.N. whom I here hold by the hand, and I receive her as my legitimate wife, and I swear never to leave her: not for someone better, or richer, or more beautiful, or more noble, or on account of any defect which God might put in her: but I swear to behave myself faithfully to her as a good husband is bound to behave to his legitimate wife, until the hour of death. Thus may God help me, and all his saints.

The woman makes the same vow in exactly the same terms, simply switching "wife" for "husband. "[59] Other forms demanded explicit renunciation of all others, and pushed hard that all marriages be publicly blessed in order to prevent ambiguous unions.[60]

In virtually all liturgies which proceeded to a Eucharist, the epistle reading was 1 Corinthians 6:15-20. That reading condemned resort to a prostitute, on grounds of the unity between Christ and the church mirrored in marriage. It ended with the exhortation: "You are not your own; you were bought at a price. Therefore honor God with your body."

In many orders for the nuptial mass, the priest gave the Peace to the married couple, but they did not then pass it to others. In a clear sign of exclusivity, another cleric received the Peace from the priest and spread it to the rest of the assembly.[61]

God's Blessing

Third, all forms declared the marriage blessed, not so much by church or priest, parents or king, but by God. Marriage was God's work based on God's word, and it was to God that the couple came for the grace to live what they had promised. The medieval church did not consider marriage as its own creature, which it could modify at will.

None of the medieval service books which I have surveyed contain any provision for blessing any sexual relationship other than a form of celibacy or the lifelong marriage of a woman and a man.[62]

Penance and the Penitentials

Penance was another medieval sacramental event which commonly included sexual matters. The very complex development of penance between the fifth century and the thirteenth cannot be sketched here. In the early middle ages, however, books called "penitentials" offered guidance for confessors (usually monastic), who needed to know the penalties properly assigned to people repenting of specific sins. All of the penitentials contained extensive lists of sexual sins, among many others. Few of them show much interest in acts that occurred within marriage, but in varying ways they catalogued and differentiated between an impressive array of acts outside of marriage. In the penitential of Columbanus, for example, the act of sodomy required the same penance as that for murder: ten years of severe ascetic restrictions. Frequent fornication required seven years; one act of fornication, three. These penalties were for monastics. For layfolk, the same sins were listed, but the penalties are somewhat less severe. Some penitentials had special rules for boys, with even lighter penances.[63]

Clearly the writers and users of these books meant to bring a varied, recalcitrant population to follow traditional Christian standards, but found the ancient church's severe means of enforcement unhelpful. As the middle ages continued, and annual confession to a priest became universal and mandatory, confessors' manuals became more concerned with helping penitents to tell all of their sinful acts and to discover the sinful dispositions behind the acts. Sexual acts outside of marriage were included among the many sins to be explored.[64] The view that the medieval church was *in principle* tolerant of such activity will not survive the reading of any of these sources.

It is clear, however, that the enforcement of those traditional standards depended on circumstances. In practice a higher standard of physical chastity was expected among Aelred's Cistercians at Rievaulx (even as they cultivated intense, loving male friendships), than among the itinerant journeymen of many crafts, who were forbidden by their guilds to marry. Those who fell into sin were expected yearly to make their confessions and communions.

> *Clearly the writers and users of these books meant to bring a varied, recalcitrant population to follow traditional Christian standards . . .*

CHAPTER

5

Episcopalians have been in the midst of a debate about the status of gay and lesbian persons since the mid-1970s. Every General Convention since 1976 has adopted resolutions on the subject. The House of Bishops, which meets independently in those years in which the General Convention is not in session, adopted resolutions of its own in 1977 and 1990.

Clerical Morality and Moral Discourse

Robert W. Prichard

The discussion has not, of course, been limited to the General Convention or the House of Bishops. Individual dioceses have conducted their own studies, the Presiding Bishop and his Council of Advice have issued statements, the church press has closely followed a growing debate, and the secular press has shown—particularly following the highly publicized ordinations to the priesthood of lesbian Ellen Barrett (1977) and gay male Robert Williams (1989)—an unaccustomed interest in the church's deliberations.

Many people have been frustrated by the "untidiness" of this recent debate. It hasn't, they note, progressed in a logical pattern. There seems to be no agreed upon starting point for the discussion. When General Convention or the House of Bishops does act, people disagree about the significance of the decisions reached. It seems appropriate, therefore, to step back from the immediate debate and ask more general questions about decision making on moral issues in the Episcopal Church. To what standards do Episcopalians look when they make determinations about clerical morality? Do those standards provide any specific guidance about gay and lesbian behavior? Are such matters left up to the individual dioceses? Does the General Convention have a role to play? This chapter attempts to answer these questions.

Standards

Church debates often center around the interpretation of certain agreed-upon texts. It seems reasonable to begin, then, with written texts that serve as standards for clerical morality in the Episcopal Church.

Scripture

Clearly Scripture is chief among the standards. Every bishop, priest, and deacon testifies to that priority at the time of ordination by declaring belief that "the Holy Scriptures of the Old and New Testaments [are] the Word of God, and . . . contain all things necessary to salvation."[65]

> *Clearly Scripture is chief among the standards. Every bishop, priest, and deacon testifies to that priority at the time of ordination . . .*

Of all the passages of Scripture associated with Anglican ordination rites, 1 Timothy 3 has been the most visible. Thomas Crammer's first ordinal (1550) included it in the rites of ordination for bishops, priests, and deacons. The chapter describes qualities to be sought and avoided when selecting bishops and deacons. Prominent among the qualities to be sought is heterosexual marital fidelity: "Now a bishop must be above reproach, the husband of one wife. . . . Let deacons be the husband of one wife . . . ." (1 Timothy 3:2, 12, RSV). Recognizing that the passage referred specifically to deacons and bishops, but not to presbyters, the revisers of the prayer book dropped the lesson from the ordination of priests in 1662.[66] It has been retained in the remaining two ordination offices to this day.

The ordination declaration affirms not only Scripture as an authority, however, for it goes on to require conformity "to the doctrine, discipline and worship of the [Protestant] Episcopal Church [in the United States of America]."[67] Since another chapter deals with biblical authority and sexual ethics, this chapter will examine in greater detail the requirement to conform to Episcopal doctrine, discipline, and worship.

Ordination Offices

The prayer book ordination offices refer to the moral character of ordinands at four specific points. These references have changed only slightly since the adoption of the first ordinal in 1550.

A Manner of Life Suitable to the Exercise of Ministry. The first reference is found in the charge to the presenters of a candidate for the diaconate. In the original 1550 ordinal the bishop said, "take heede that the persones whom ye present unto us, be apte and meete, for theyr learning, and godlye conversation . . . ."[68] This charge, which was added to the ordination of priests in 1662, remained unchanged through 1928. The 1979 prayer book rendered the expression "godly conversation" as "a manner of life . . . suitable to the exercise of this ministry."[69]

Impediments or Crimes. A second reference to clerical morality occurs in the inquiry directed to the congregation about the fitness of the ordinand. It is similar to the charge to the congregation following the exhortation in the marriage service. In 1550 the bishop asked the congregation at the ordination of a deacon or priest "yf there bee anye of you, who knoweth anye impediemente, or notable crime, in any of these persones presented . . . for whiche he ought not to be admitted to the same."[70] The 1979 prayer book continues to ask about any such impediment or crime and also introduces a parallel inquiry into the ordination of bishops.

Wholesome Examples. This third reference is found in the examination of the candidate. In 1550 deacons and priests were asked whether they would "applye all youre diligence to frame and fasshion youre owne lyves, and the lives of all youre familie, according to the doctrine of Christ, and to make bothe yourselves and them as muche as in you lieth, wholesome examples of the flocke of Christ?" Bishops were asked whether they would "deny all ungodlynesse, and worldly lustes, and live soberly, righteously, and Godly in this worlde . . . ?"[71] In the 1979 prayer book priests and deacons are still called upon to provide wholesome examples. The inquiry has, however, been dropped from the ordination of bishops.

Holiness of Life. Finally, one or more prayers ask God to grant particular qualities to the ordinand. From 1550 through 1928 prayers asked that deacons, priests, and bishops might have "innocency of life." A closing prayer for bishops asked God that the newly ordained bishop be a "wholesome example, in word, in conversation, in love, in faith, in chastity, and in purity," a phrase that disappeared as part of the reworking of the final prayers in the 1979 prayer book.[72] The 1979 *Book of Common Prayer* has rendered "innocency of life" as "holiness of life."[73]

The *Book of Common Prayer* thus has provided some of the vocabulary that is being used in the current debate in the church. Clergy are to have "a manner of life . . . suitable to the exercise of . . . ministry." They are to be free of "crime or impediment," to serve as "wholesome examples," and, with God's assistance, to exhibit "holiness of life."

Constitution and Canons

The canons of the church on clerical morality have been shaped primarily as a commentary upon the words of the ordination offices. The church, the canons imply, takes the ordination offices seriously. A canon, which was first adopted in 1789, requires a signed testimonial from the Standing Committee indicating that candidates for ordination have lived "a sober, honest, and godly life."[74] Other canons made it clear that the church expected clergy to continue exhibiting the qualities that were required of them in order to be ordained. The seventy-fifth English canon of 1604 and the thirteenth American canon of 1789 were titled "Sober Conversation required in Ministers."[75] The canons spelled out in detail a few of the implications of the "conversation" expected of clergy.

The General Conventions of 1829 and 1832 reshaped and retitled the American canon more along the lines of the inquiry about "crime or impediment." The reworked canon's title was "Of Offenses for which Ministers shall be Tried and Punished," and the first such offenses listed was "any crime or gross immorality."[76] The canon of 1832 did include some of the specific details of behavior of the earlier 1789 canon, but these were dropped in an 1868 revision that left the simple formula "crime or immorality" as the basis for trial. In 1883 an addition to the canon explicitly required the Standing Committee to conduct an inquiry of any clergy "convicted in any court of record, of any crime or misdemeanor involving immorality, or against whom a judgment has been duly recorded in any court of record, in a case involving immorality."[77]

The church expects "a sober, honest, and godly life" in those seeking ordination.

While successive General Conventions have wrestled with the theological offenses and the breaches of discipline for which a cleric might be tried, the language concerning the personal morality of clergy has remained unchanged since the General Convention of 1883. The church expects "a sober, honest, and godly life" in those seeking ordination. An "impediment or crime" is sufficient cause to halt an ordination. "Crime or immorality" is a sufficient cause for ecclesiastical trial.

Sexual Morality

The ordination offices in the *Book of Common Prayer* and the canons of the church are the written standards for clergy behavior. Do they say anything specific about fornication, adultery, or homosexuality? They have in fact said very little. Outside of the 1550-1928 closing prayer for chastity in the ordination of bishops and the biblical lessons specified, there have been no specific definitions of clerical sexual morality in the ordination offices or canons.

One can quickly locate more specific language in the marriage office and canons, the ten commandments, and the Sunday and daily lectionaries, but in doing so one must not overlook the basic character of canons in the Episcopal Church. There is no specific canon condemning sexual relations outside of heterosexual marriage for clergy, because Episcopal canons have never been an exhaustive code of behavior. Episcopalians and other Anglicans in the world generally do not follow such examples as Roman Law or the Napoleonic Code. They do not construct intricate systems of morality and ethics that cover every eventuality. Rather, in the English common law tradition, Episcopalians have been content with a few basic principles, a body of laws drafted to deal with a few difficult circumstances, and an accumulated history of judicial decisions.[78]

Understanding the common law character of Episcopal canon law can help us find the contours of moral debate in the denomination. Absence of specific prohibition, for one thing, does not constitute approval.[79] One cannot conclude, for example, that the lack of any specific canonical prohibition against clerical murder is an invitation for clergy to moonlight as professional assassins.

Maintaining Sexual Discipline

Although the General Convention has adopted the *Book of Common Prayer* and the canons governing clerical behavior, the responsibility for actually monitoring the behavior of priests and deacons and administering discipline falls to the individual dioceses.[80] It is a weighty responsibility.

It is difficult, because such proceedings are confidential, to gain a precise picture of the number of disciplinary actions and ecclesiastical trials. The triennial reports of the Recorder of Ordinations on the number of persons removed from the ministry would suggest, however, that the enforcement of discipline is a responsibility that dioceses exercise with some regularity.[81] This figure averaged 71 a triennium for the period between the conventions of 1949 and 1971. It rose to 123 a triennium between the conventions of 1971 and 1982, but fell to an average of 100 from 1982 to 1988.[82] Therefore, 20 to 40 clergy face some judicial trial or action each year somewhere in the church.

> . . . 20 to 40 clergy face some judicial trial or action each year somewhere in the church.

The church has no clearly established procedure for compiling the results of this judicial process. The proceedings of notable trials, such as that in 1844 of Bishop Benjamin T. Onderdonk of New York for sexual harassment of female members of clergy families, are published, but in most cases the details of church trials are kept secret. In addition, many bishops, despite a canon to the contrary, allow clergy suspected of moral offenses to renounce their orders in order to avoid a presentment.[83] Informal conversations with bishops, diocesan chancellors, members of church courts, and others acquainted with the deposition process suggest, however, the following:

1. If one discounts the short term increase in depositions and removals from the ordained ministry in the 1970s due to dissatisfaction with prayer book revision and the ordination of women, the primary long term cause for removals from the ministry is clerical immorality.

2. Although some presentments are based upon alleged fiscal dishonesty, the primary cause for charges of clerical immorality is sexual misconduct.

3. Both heterosexual and homosexual immorality is involved, usually of a rather blatant kind.[84]

One can thus trace a history in the Episcopal Church, not only of prayer book and canonical prescriptions for clerical morality, but also of a judicial attempt to use that standard to exclude sexual relationships outside of marriage.

Leadership from General Convention

The prayer book and canons speak of wholesome examples, godly lives, and holiness of life. Dioceses have regularly interpreted that standard to exclude sexual relationships outside of marriage. But, one may well ask, how is the church to respond when individual dioceses begin to interpret the standard in novel ways? Obviously, that is what has begun to happen in the last 15 years. Some have begun to redefine "wholesome example" to include those who engage in sexual relations (both heterosexual and homosexual) outside of marriage. What has the church done in such circumstances in the past?

The answer is relatively simple. In the past Episcopalians have done roughly what they are doing at present. They have, in effect, asked for advice and clarification from the General Convention, which has in return responded with pastoral letters, resolutions, and in rare cases, short-term changes in the canons. Three examples may make this pattern more clear. The first concerns alcoholism, the second dueling, and the third "amusements."

Alcoholism

In the early years following the American Revolution alcoholism was a major problem. Few of the social conventions and legal constraints of today existed at that time. Young children were served alcohol, political candidates encouraged voters by serving free drinks on election day, and employees took morning alcohol breaks in much the same way that workers today break for coffee. The per capita consumption of alcohol was three times that of modern America.[85]

> *Smith was an able administrator, a respected educator, a key leader in the formation of the General Convention, and an alcoholic.*

An election in the Diocese of Maryland brought the issue home to the General Convention with particular force. The Episcopalians in Maryland elected Dr. William Smith (1727-1803) as their bishop.[86] Smith was an able administrator, a respected educator, a key leader in the formation of the General Convention, and an alcoholic.

The election presented the deputies and bishops at General Convention with a problem. The English had always understood alcoholism as an undesirable quality in clergy. The English canons under which American Anglicans had lived during the colonial era explicitly condemned clerical drunkenness. With the Revolution, however, Americans lacked any canons of their own. The members of General Convention, whose consent was required before consecration, initially tried to resolve the problem by ignoring Smith's election.[87] They approved candidates elected in New York, Pennsylvania, and Virginia, but took no action on Maryland's bishop-elect.

With the adoption of the first canons in 1789, however, the General Convention took another step. Reaching back into their English heritage, they reproduced language from the English canon of

1604. "No ecclesiastical persons shall, other than for their honest necessities," the canon that the Americans adopted on sober conversation read, "resort to tavern or other places most liable to be abused to licentiousness. Further, they shall not give themselves . . . to drinking and riot."[88] The canon included other elements from the English canon, but not all. The Americans of 1789 did not, for example, feel the need to adopt the language from the English canons concerning "dice, cards, or tables."[89]

The language against alcoholism remained in the canons until 1829, when it and other specifics were replaced with the general formula "scandalous, disorderly, or immoral conduct." Some members of General Convention apparently felt this action premature, for in 1832 they restored a specific reference to "drunkenness." This reference was retained until 1868, when it was replaced by the general formula "crime or immorality."[90]

Dueling

The General Convention chose to deal with the problem of dueling with a resolution rather than a canon. Dueling, like alcoholism, was a rising problem in the early years after the American Revolution. Not only celebrated figures such as Vice President Aaron Burr and President Andrew Jackson, but also a number of lesser figures killed men in duels.

Clergy, who were often summoned to attend the losing party in duels, faced difficult pastoral problems. How should they react to requests to administer communion to or to preside at the funerals of those who died as a result of dueling? Bishop Benjamin Moore of New York faced one such quandary in 1804, when called to the bedside of Alexander Hamilton. Walter Addison, a Maryland clergyman with a parish near the dueling grounds for Washington, D. C., faced a similar difficulty.[91] Clergyman James Milnor knew the problem as well; shortly before entering the ordained ministry he was challenged to a duel.

The bishops and deputies who gathered in General Convention in 1808 decided to act upon the problem by adopting a simple resolution: "Ministers of this Church ought not to perform the funeral services, in the case of any person who shall give or accept a challenge to a duel."[92] Three years later the bishops and deputies at convention revised their position by adopting a statement declaring that "the resolution passed by the last Convention, on the subject of dueling, be considered as not precluding any Minister from performing the burial service, when the person giving or receiving a challenge has afterwards exhibited evidence of sincere repentance."[93]

The 1808 statement and its revision, though never a part of canon law or the ordination offices, provided a specific commentary on the godly life that clergy were expected to uphold. Such a life was not to include dueling, and those guilty of such behavior needed to repent before regaining the ministrations of the church.

Amusements

In 1817 the bishops of the church dealt with a moral problem in a third way: They issued a pastoral letter. The problem that concerned the bishops was the rising popularity of forms of amusement that they felt unsuitable. English canon law contained no specific precedents for censuring most of the activities, though an occasional English clerical manual had expressed disapproval.[94] The bishops were treading, therefore, on somewhat new ground when they adopted a resolution and issued a pastoral letter cautioning against gambling, "amusements involving cruelty to the brute creation" (in other words, cock fighting and dog fighting), and attending the theater.[95]

These three examples indicate some of the ways Episcopalians have met moral crises in the past. Although the administration of clerical discipline is in the hands of the individual dioceses, the General Convention has provided the leadership on new and vexing challenges to the understanding of what it means to serve as a "wholesome example" or to live a "godly life."

The Current Debate

Since 1976 Episcopalians have been engaged in a process surprisingly like the General Convention's earlier debates over alcohol, dueling, and amusements. Prior to 1976, few in the church questioned the appropriateness of the traditional standard of sexual morality. (Most of the laity of the church, who oppose "the sanctioning by the Episcopal Church of relationships between members of the same sex" by a more than three to one margin, continue to support the traditional standard.[96])

Once groups such as Integrity and individual bishops such as

Paul Moore and John S. Spong began to question that standard, however, those who are responsible for monitoring clerical behavior in the individual dioceses turned to General Convention for clarification. The General Convention as a whole and the House of Bishops in particular have responded with a series of resolutions. Such resolutions do not carry the authority of the prayer book or of the canons, but reliance upon them does conform with the way that Episcopalians have dealt with moral crises in the past. The following review of these resolutions may be helpful.

The 1976 General Convention Resolution

The 1976 General Convention recognized that homosexual persons were "children of God who have a full and equal claim with all other persons upon the love, acceptance, and pastoral concern and care of the church."[97] This statement, which was reaffirmed by the General Conventions of 1979, 1982, 1985, and 1988, has framed the subsequent debate in the church. All involved in the debate since 1976 have shared this common starting point.

The debate about the appropriateness of the ordination and marriage of active gay men and lesbians has not been a debate about whether persons should have access to pastoral care or membership in the church. It has been a debate about a morality of a behavior. Are those who engage in homosexual activity like those (to use some of Paul's examples from Romans 1) who gossip, slander, or disobey their parents? Or is their behavior one that the church should bless and raise up as a wholesome example?

The 1977 Resolution of the House of Bishops

When some (including Bishop Paul Moore, Jr. of New York, who ordained Integrity co-president Ellen Barrett to the priesthood in 1977) interpreted the 1976 statement as a movement toward acceptance of homosexual behavior, the House of Bishops responded by adopting a statement declaring that

> The Biblical understanding rejects homosexual practice. Heterosexual sex is clearly and repeatedly affirmed as God's will for humanity. The teaching of Jesus about marriage, the teaching of Paul and other Biblical writers are unanimous and undeviating in portraying heterosexual love as God's will and therefore good and normative at the same

time keeping in mind our Lord's recognition (cf. Matthew 19:12) that there is also virtue in the celibate life. It is clear from Scripture that heterosexual marriage is unanimously affirmed and that homosexual activity is condemned. It is not clear from Scripture just what morality attaches to homosexual orientation, but the Christian message of redemption and sanctification is one of graceful acceptance leading to graceful wholeness for all people.

The Church, therefore, is right to confine its nuptial blessing exclusively to heterosexual marriage. Homosexual unions witness to incompleteness. For the Church to institutionalize by liturgical action a relationship that violates its own teaching about sex is inadmissible.

With respect to the question of ordaining homosexuals it is crucial to distinguish between (a) an advocating and/or practicing—willful and habitual—homosexual and, (b) one with a dominant homosexual orientation only.

"The ordination of an advocating and/or practicing homosexual, therefore, involves the Church in a public denial of its own theological and moral norms on sexuality."

In the case of an advocating and/or practicing homosexual, ordination is inadmissible. First, because ordination is a corporate act which proclaims our understanding of ministry, the Church thereby sets forth its values, not simply for itself, but in evangelistic terms for the social order. The ordination of an advocating and/or practicing homosexual, therefore, involves the Church in a public denial of its own theological and moral norms on sexuality.

Second, one of the vows required of an ordinand commits him or her to the fashioning of personal (and family or community) life after the manner of Christ so as to be an example to the Church.

The ordination of an advocating and/or practicing homosexual would require the Church's sanction of such a life style, not only as acceptable, but worthy of emulation. Our present understanding of Biblical and theological truth would make this impossible.[98]

That is to say, the bishops responded to a novel interpretation of sexual ethics by referring to Scripture, the ordination office, and the tradition of the church, all of which they believed rejected the marriage and ordination of those with active homosexual behavior.

The 1979 General Convention Resolution

The General Convention of 1979 adopted a related proposal, with an explicit awareness of the relationship of the action to the diocesan responsibility for clerical morality. The convention understood its action as a recommendation "to Bishops, Pastors, Vestries, Commissions on Ministry and Standing Committees . . . as they continue to exercise their proper canonical functions in the selection and approval of persons for ordination." The resolution that followed recalled the prayer book language about wholesome examples, reaffirmed "the traditional teaching of the Church on marriage, marital fidelity and sexual chastity as the standard of Christian sexual morality," and declared the belief that it was "not appropriate for this Church to ordain a practicing homosexual, or any person who is engaged in heterosexual relations outside of marriage."[99]

The 1988 General Convention repeated the affirmation of "the Biblical and traditional teaching on chastity and fidelity in personal relationships." It also listed a series of supplements to "the accepted sources of authority for Christians, namely Scripture, tradition, reason and experience." The 1979 General Convention resolution was included among those supplements, as were the 1976, 1982, and 1985 resolutions on the status of homosexual persons in the church.[100]

The English General Synod Statements of 1987 and 1991

As was the case in the past century, some Americans have looked to the English for confirmation of their understanding of the tradition of the church. The English General Synod of 1987 adopted a statement that paralleled the American statements of 1977 and 1979. The English statement read:

> This Synod affirms that the Biblical and traditional teaching on chastity and fidelity in personal relationships is a

response to and expression of God's love for each of us, and in particular affirms:

1. that sexual intercourse is an act of total commitment which belongs properly within a permanent marriage relationship;

2. that fornication and adultery are sins against this ideal, and are to be met by a call to repentance and the exercise of compassion;

3. that homosexual acts also fall short of this ideal, and are likewise to be met by a call to repentance and the exercise of compassion;

4. that all Christians are called to be exemplary in all spheres of morality, including sexual morality, and that holiness of life is particularly required for Christian leaders.[101]

The 1988 General Convention listing of supplements to the accepted sources of authority for Christians included the 1987 General Synod statement. A group of 52 American bishops made their agreement with it more explicit by signing a declaration of endorsement.[102]

In December of 1991 the House of Bishops of the General Synod of the Church of England issued a comprehensive statement titled *Issues in Human Sexuality.* This document explored the pastoral implications of the church's traditional teaching on homosexuality and attempted to strike a balance between two "fundamental principles." The first was:

> that homophile orientation and its expression in sexual activity do not constitute a parallel and alternative form of human sexuality as complete within the terms of the created order as the heterosexual. The convergence of Scripture, tradition and reasoned reflection on experience, even including the newly sympathetic and perceptive thinking of our own day, make it impossible for the Church to come with integrity to any other conclusion. Heterosexuality and homosexuality are not equally congruous with the observed order of creation or with the insights of revelation as the Church engages with these in the light of her pastoral ministry.[103]

The bishops' second fundamental principle was that "homosexual people are in every way as valuable to and as valued by God as heterosexual people."[104]

The bishops applied these two principles to a variety of pastoral situations and made specific recommendations. Among them were the following, which are numbered to correspond to the subsections of chapter five:

5. "Christian homophiles . . . who witness to God's general will for human sexuality by a life of abstinence . . . [deserve] all praise and support of the Church members through prayer, understanding and active friendship."

6. The church is unable to "commend the way of life" of those "who are conscientiously convinced that this way of abstinence is not the best for them, and that they have more hope of growing in love for God and neighbour with the help of a loving and faithful homophile partnership, in intention lifelong, where mutual self-giving includes the physical expression of their attachment." Nonetheless since "the Christian tradition also contains an emphasis on respect for free conscientious judgement where the individual has seriously weighed the issues involved . . . [the bishops] do not reject those who sincerely believe it is God's call to them. [The bishops] stand alongside them in the fellowship of the Church, all alike dependent upon the undeserved grace of God."

7. This acceptance "no more countenances promiscuous, casual or exploitative sex for the homophile than for the heterophile. The ideal of chastity holds good for all Christians; and homophiles who do not renounce all physical sex relations must nevertheless be guided by some form of that ideal appropriate to them."

8. "Bisexual activity must always be wrong for this reason, if for no other, than it inevitably involves being unfaithful."

9. The "argument . . . that the norm of a faithful one-to-one relationship—dismissed as 'coupledom'—is simply an alien legacy from the heterophile world within its family and social responsibilities [and that] by contrast the homophile can and should enjoy the freedom to express through physical sex a whole range of relationships, profound or superficial, transient

or longer lasting, with any number of partners . . . is simply a pretentious disguise for the evil of promiscuity."

10. That "paedophilia breaches the limits of what is right and healthy in the child-adult relationship, and in Christian terms is a sin not only against chastity but against charity and justice." The bishops note, however, that "a homophile orientation does not, any more than a heterophile, of itself entail a sexual interest in or attraction to children." Therefore, "it is mistaken and unjust to assume . . . that children in school or in a church choir are particularly at risk from gay or lesbian members of staff."

11. "Many homophile clergy are highly dedicated and have been greatly blessed."

13. "From the time of the New Testament onwards it has been expected of those appointed to the ministry of authority in the Church that they not only preach but live the Gospel. . . . People not only inside the Church but outside it believe rightly that in the way of life of an ordained minister, they ought to see a pattern which the Church commends. . . . This means that certain possibilities are not open to the clergy by comparison with the laity. . . ."

16. "The Ordinal of 1662 and the Canon law do indeed require those ordained deacon and priest to make both themselves and their families wholesome examples and patterns to the flock of Christ."

17. "The clergy cannot claim the liberty to enter into sexually active homophile relationships. . . . To allow such a claim on their part would be seen as placing that way of life in all respects on a par with heterosexual marriage as a reflection of God's purposes in creation. The Church cannot accept such a parity and remain faithful to the insights which God has given it through Scripture, tradition and reasoned reflection on experience."

18. It is grossly unfair "to regard any two people of the same sex who choose to make their home together as being in some form of erotic relationship." The Church of England should continue "to trust its members, and not to carry out intrusive interrogations in order to make sure that they are behaving themselves." The bishops will continue "to treat all clergy who give no occa-

sion for scandal with trust and respect, and . . . expect all . . . fellow Christians to do the same."

19. "Those clergy who feel it their duty to come out, that is, to make known publicly . . . that they are homophile in orientation, but . . . are committed to a life of abstinence [present no problem to anyone]."

21. The bishops "call upon all clergy to live lives that respect the Church's teaching, and . . . [will] do everything in [their] power to help them to do so."

22. "Candidates for ordination also must be prepared to abide by the same standards." However, the bishops "do not think it right to interrogate individuals on their sexual lives, unless there are strong reasons for doing so. Ordinarily it should be left to candidates' own consciences to act responsibly in this matter."

24. If Christians are "faithful to Our Lord, then disagreements over the proper expression of homosexual love will never become rejection of the homosexual person." [105]

The bishops characterized their position on sexuality as the "mind of the church." They recognized that some would disagree. Clergy, they said, "are free to argue for change, [but] . . . are not free . . . to go against that mind in their own practice."[106]

As of March 1992 the American House of Bishops had not yet commented upon this English statement.

Recent American Actions

In 1990 the Presiding Bishop and his Council of Advice, which is composed of the bishops who serve as presidents or vice-presidents of the nine provinces, responded to Bishop John S. Spong's ordination of gay male Robert Williams. Their statement both "disassociated" the presiding bishop and council from the ordination and reaffirmed the 1979 General Convention statement.[107] The House of Bishops, in turn, voted to "affirm and support" that statement at its September 1990 meeting.[108]

The question of human sexuality was again debated at the 1991 General Convention. The bishops and deputies at the convention considered three significant proposals:

1. *The Standing Commission on Human Affairs or Hunt resolution.* The commission is a nine-member body that meets between sessions of the Convention in order to consider and make proposals about issues that the Convention refers to it. Bishop George N. Hunt of Rhode Island, who chaired the commission, and six of the commission's remaining eight members favored rejection of the 1979 Convention position and open acceptance of some level of homosexual activity. The commission's report recommended a study of "the theological and liturgical issues involved in affirming and blessing . . . covenants of gay and lesbian persons" and recommended the ordination of "gay men and lesbians otherwise qualified who display the same integrity in their sexual relationships which we ask of our heterosexual ordinands." Aware, however, of the unlikelihood of approval in either house of General Convention, the commission did not present these recommendations in a form that allowed for a direct vote. Instead, the commission crafted a resolution suggesting that the General Convention was the wrong forum in which to make determinations about the fitness of gay and lesbian persons for ordination. The committee resolution read:

> *Bishop George N. Hunt . . . and six of the commission's remaining eight members favored rejection of the 1979 Convention position and open acceptance of some level of homosexual activity.*

> *Resolved* . . . that each Diocese of this Church, acting in accordance with the Constitution and Canons of the Episcopal Church in the United States of America, and in accordance with its own constitution and canons, is fully competent to determine whom best to ordain to the ordained ministry of the Church in the light of the qualifications presented for ordinations in the Book of Common Prayer; and be it further
>
> *Resolved*, that, in accordance with national and local canons and long standing practice, the Ecclesiasti-

cal Authority in each diocese determines which clergy may be received or licensed to officiate with the respective diocese(s).[109]

Bishop Hunt argued that the adoption of this provision would "negate the 1979 resolution" of General Convention.[110] This resolution lacked sufficient support to reach the floor of either house. The House of Bishops' committee on ministry suggested a substitute resolution, which also became the basis of debate in the House of Deputies.

2. *The Frey resolution.* Bishop William Frey, the former Bishop of Colorado who is currently the Dean of Trinity Episcopal School for the Ministry, proposed a resolution, which, if passed, would have made the prohibition of sex outside of monogamous marriage an explicit matter of canon law for clergy. "All members of the clergy of this church," it read, "shall abstain from genital relationship outside of holy matrimony."[111]

While the intent of the resolution was not new—it was very much in line with the statements of 1977 and 1979—the form was; unlike previous explicit legislation it was to be a permanent part of the church's canon law, rather than a simple statement by a convention.

The Frey resolution had considerable support, but did not pass. In the House of Deputies the resolution failed in both the lay (46 dioceses for, 47 against, and 21 divided) and clerical order (43 dioceses for, 48 against, and 25 divided).[112] The bishops did not vote on the resolution directly, voting instead on the "Howe amendment," a resolution introduced by Bishop John Howe of Central Florida with the content of the Frey amendment but in the form of a resolution rather than a canon. The Howe resolution received strong support, especially from members of "the Irenaeus fellowship," an informal grouping of approximately 80 bishops that had been meeting regularly since the 1989 convention. It failed by a vote of 91 to 85.

3. *The substitute resolution drafted by the House of Bishops' Committee on Ministry.* The resolution reaffirmed the belief "that the teaching of the Episcopal Church is that physical sexual expression is appropriate only with the lifelong, monogamous 'union of husband and wife in the heart, body and

mind . . . .' "[113] The final form of the resolution, after modifications during debate, differed slightly from resolutions adopted by previous General Conventions in that it both explicitly linked this teaching to the marriage service in the *Book of Common Prayer* and recognized the "discontinuity between this teaching and the experience of many." The resolution called, in addition, for continued dialogue, and requested the House of Bishops to "prepare a Pastoral Teaching" prior to the 1994 Convention. The resolution passed easily in both houses. The bishops overwhelmingly approved the resolution, as did the lay (99 delegations for, 9 against, and 4 divided) and clerical orders (106 clerical delegations for, 5 against, and 4 divided) in the House of Deputies.[114]

The end result of the 1991 General Convention was, therefore, a continuation of the policy that dates back to the 1977 House of Bishops and the 1979 General Convention: the adoption of a resolution (but not a canon) affirming that genital relations belong within lifelong, monogamous marriage. Some would like to make such a statement a matter of canon law and others would like to adopt an entirely different standard, but to this point the General Convention has consistently refused to do either. As of this date, the statements of 1977, 1979, and 1991 provide the church's most cogent and consistent commentary upon the prayer book's ideal of wholesome clerical example.

CHAPTER

6

Pastors are often asked whether the church has anything to say about questions whose resolutions are controversial. Adults ask. Young people ask. They are confused by the complexity of the issues with which they grapple and by the lack of clearly defined answers. All these people are confused because the questions they are forced to ask are complex and lack clearly defined answers. My response has always been, "Yes. Yes, the church has something to say on controversial issues. The Christian life is free, but it is not improvised."

Speaking on Controversial Issues

Judith M. McDaniel

Inquiry about the church's position, however, implies a related question, which is often posed to a pastor: "I recognize that you as a representative of the church have a position on a controversial issue. Once you have stated it, is there anything left that you can say to me, or I to you?" This question is not trivial. Its answer, too, is always, "Yes. There is room for us to talk. We must talk."

As the authors of Chapter 2 argue, Anglicans are in some agreement about the sources that are authoritative for them. They look first to Scripture, then to tradition and reason. This chapter maintains that after we have identified what these authorities have to say on issues of controversy, we do have something left to say to one another. We can have conversations that do not dissolve into diatribe, a preacher can speak with conviction as well as compassion, and we all can listen and learn. Developments in hermeneutics suggest a helpful new perspective from which we can view the event of Christian conversation.

Hermeneutics is the study of the art of interpretation. It is the investigation of the position from which one states a claim. It leads to an awareness that each act of interpretation presupposes a theological stance. Theological conversation of necessity involves interpretation.

Scholars have understood the substance of hermeneutics in various ways during the past two centuries. Over this time, the definition of hermeneutics has shifted from the study of theories of interpretation to the study of meaning itself. Current hermeneutical theory presumes that neither "side" in a conversation about meaning possesses the whole truth. The truth is larger than the perspective of either partner to a dialogue.

Christians define themselves and all things by their relationship to God. That convenantal relationship, that bond of faith and grace between God and believing humanity, holds promise for all of our struggling attempts to communicate with one another. When we are grounded in that primary relationship between ourselves and God, we can step forward to speak together on controversial issues, for we have hope. How, then, shall a new hermeneutic proceed?

> *The truth is larger than the perspective of either partner to a dialogue.*

A new hermeneutic will not advance by using Scripture against Scripture. Pointing out the conflicts between the infancy narratives of Matthew and Luke, or numerous other conflicting accounts of events in biblical times, places reason on an equal footing with Scripture.[115] That is, when we place passages in contrast in order to judge them, we are not simply making a comparison, but imposing an external criteria on Scripture—human reason.

This does not mean that critical exegesis has no place; on the contrary, it is valuable for helping us understand the intention of the authors of the biblical text. *But the interpretation of the author's intention is not the whole story.* The truth beneath the words of the text is authoritative. The principles behind the individual biblical author's contextualized choice of vocabulary hold the truth, and a new hermeneutic seeks that truth.

A Positivist Hermeneutic

Christian preaching tells a particular story, the good news that God was in Christ. Unfortunately, many people have objectified God. The danger of reducing God to an object of investigation is evident in the methodology and goals of much biblical exegesis.

If Scripture were just another record of human cultural advance, it could be scientifically critiqued and tested against physical reality. But such a view tends to dissolve the meaning of Scripture into its immediate context. This reduces the Word of God to the realm of scientific advance, undermines the authority of the biblical message, and makes the idea of providential guidance problematic. Scientific analysis reduces Christian Scripture to its historical origins, literary roots, and contextual demands, concentrating on sources of tradition, units of oral transmission, and the biblical authors' intentions. This approach breaks the scriptural text into its constituent parts and dissipates the Bible's authority. The search for positive knowledge based on natural phenomena, which are verifiable by the empirical sciences, replaces the language of salvation. This is a positivist hermeneutic.

The primary problem with a positivist hermeneutic of this nature is theological: It sets up a subject-object dichotomy that forces us to talk about, but not with, God. It limits God and the power of God's creative presence in our lives. It presumes that the use of literary, textual, source, form, historical, and redaction criticism tells us the truth about Jesus the Christ.

Fortunately, alternatives to such a positivist hermeneutic exist. Although clarified by recent thought, the roots of such alternatives are quite old. One particularly fruitful approach is to consider the meaning of texts in the context of the community that reads them. Centuries ago, classic Christian authors such as Augustine of Hippo and Vincent of Lerins began to explore the ways in which a community's assent to a religious proposition testified to its trustworthiness.[116]

Generations of Christians of a mystical bent—from Pseudo-Dionysius to Bonaventure to the Cambridge Platonists—shared a second important hermeneutical insight: Truth may not be easily reducible to logical propositions.

In the nineteenth century, John Henry Newman used the art of rhetoric to make the same observation. Rhetoric as an art has ancient and venerable roots. Its principal vehicle of investigation was topical reasoning. Newman used topical reasoning in *An Essay on the Development of Christian Doctrine*.[117]

Topical reasoning is particularly useful in debating controversial issues. It places contrasting pairs of terms in opposition and does not seek to find a third term that will reconcile them. Instead, topical reasoning maintains the contrast and comparison inherent in placing the opposite terms in juxtaposition.

Topical reasoning requires an active mind capable of seeking organizing principles without predetermining the outcome of the "argument" that arises when the conflicting ideas are placed side by side. Topics are "seats" of argument, not *the* argument. They are open spaces from which to take a stance. Topical reasoning proceeds as we recognize indeterminacy and uncertainty.

Newman's genius lay in recognizing that because we share the assumptions of truth behind each of the opposite terms, we can hold their contingent claims in tension. This allows us to strongly agree with the weight of accumulated evidence about the terms.[118]

The apostle Paul used topical reasoning, as any well-educated person of his day would have. For example, he wrote that there is neither Jew nor Greek, male nor female, slave nor free in the church —all are one in Jesus Christ (see Galatians 3:28). Paul recognized that truth resides outside the contrast of what appear to be opposites. Belonging to each other is needed for the oneness between Christ and his church to be made real.

Twentieth-Century Insights

Twentieth-century authors in the field of hermeneutics have wrestled with the same basic problem that Paul and Newman confronted—how can we reach conclusions in the relatively indeterminate field of religion? Contemporary authors may use different terminology and metaphors, but they share with Newman a deep awareness that religious argumentation proceeds by something other than the logical construction of syllogisms. In particular, such twentieth-century biblical, theological, and philosophical scholars as Martin Heidegger, Rudolph Bultmann, Helmut Thielicke, Paul Ricoeur, and Hans-Georg Gadamer—and authors who build upon their insights such as Calvin Schrag, John Stewart, Richard Palmer, Richard Lischer, and Barbara Warnick—argue that human conversation is revelatory.[119] For them, speaking is the matrix of relationship in which Being is disclosed and new meaning emerges.

Women and men bring themselves, their values, and their own histories —what Hans-Georg Gadamer calls their horizons—to any conversation . . .

This focus on language as a means of revelation leads us to consider the way we should view the event of Christian preaching. Certainly Scripture contains a kernel of the meaning of Jesus the Christ. Preaching bears witness to that truth, but it is more complex than that. Rudolph Bultmann referred to preaching as *kerygma*—both the act of proclaiming the message and the subject of that preaching. Combining the act of communication with its subject is the concern of contemporary hermeneutics.

Calvin O. Schrag has described action and conversation as "complementary moments of expressive meaning."[120] He explains that communication is about something, by someone, to another person. The "about" of biblical hermeneutics is the news of Jesus the Christ as found in the canon of Scripture. The "by" and "to" of Schrag's description point to the social nature of shared understanding. Women and men bring themselves, their values, and their own histories—what Hans-Georg Gadamer calls their horizons—to any conversation in which they participate. While those elements can make understanding difficult, they also create the potential for new truths and insights that were not part of the horizon of the original authors of the text under discussion. Paul Ricoeur calls this characteristic of conversation "a surplus of meaning."[121]

The idea that a text or act of communication has a surplus of meaning suggests that the task for hermeneutics is not to restore the horizon of the author but, rather, to integrate the author's horizon with our own. When we do this, we attain what John Stewart calls "a higher universality that overcomes, not only our own particularity, but also that of the other."[122] Such a fusion of horizons is only possible if the speaker enters into a conversational relationship with the biblical text to constitute a world rather than represent a world long past.[123] To do this the speaker must believe that truth is more than knowledge or methodology.

Understanding a text requires a "fusion of horizons," a blending of meanings from disparate times and places.

Hans-Georg Gadamer explains that, "We belong to language and history; we participate in them." But participation in a text "means that one does not seek to become master of what is in the text but to become the 'servant' of the text; one doesn't so much try to observe and see what is in the text as to follow, participate in, and 'hear' what is said by the text."[124] Thus, understanding a text requires a "fusion of horizons," a blending of meanings from disparate times and places.

The speaker's encounter with the text reveals a new world; the world of the speaker's experience as illuminated by the "governing claim of the text."[125] The speaker/interpreter must "appropriate the text's meaning . . . [and] move beyond the text's sense to its reference in the lived experience of the receiver."[126] That appropriation becomes a world "in front of" the text. Richard Palmer explains:

> The keys to understanding are not manipulation and control but participation and openness, not knowledge but experience, not methodology but dialectic.[127]

Paraphrasing Gadamer, Richard Palmer further explains that, "The interpretation of a text, then, is not passive openness but dialectical interaction with the text; it is not bald reenactment but a new creation, a new event in understanding."[128]

Thus, the rhetorical turn toward the other speaker is *kerygma,* the mingling of the act of speaking with its subject matter or text. Proclamation must still "serve" the meaning of the text, and the speaker/

interpreter must risk her or his "own position to place it in the light of the governing claim of the text."[129] The one who proclaims sends forth the interpretation, which is at the same time a mutual lived event, in a form that may be engaged by the hearers.

To "send" the message to another person does not mean the speaker distances herself or himself from that communication. The speaker must remain present in that communication in order to "sculpt mutual meanings."[130]

The Role of the Spirit

Martin Buber's use of the term "spirit" can help us focus attention on the connection between speaker and hearer. John Stewart explains:

> From Buber's perspective, "spirit" is not to be understood as the breath of life God breathes into human nostrils. Instead, one important meaning of the term "spirit" is, roughly speaking, turn-toward-ability, the inclination and capacity to encounter another person as other and as person . . . . "Spirit is not in the I but between I and You."[131]

How, then, does this characterization of conversation as an event between speaker and hearer relate to the basic theological motifs of the Judeo-Christian tradition?

Richard Lischer has noted a theme similar to Buber's in the work of the theologian Helmut Thielicke. As a Christian Thielicke goes beyond Buber's reference to the spirit to talk of the third person of the Trinity. Lischer explains:

> Thielicke . . . calls the Spirit the great Hermeneut whose work of spanning the distance between God and humankind serves as a protest against the divorce of subject and object.[132]

Buber looked to "spirit" and Thielicke to "the Spirit" as the one who provides the power to move into that new experience of meaning and creates the communicative event. In the Spirit's presence and power, the speaker and listener invoke memory to interpret, not simply reproduce, the text.

In the movement toward meaning the Spirit opens us to new

experiences and, thus, to new reality. The preacher who stands in the pulpit or the Christian who participates in dialogue is, therefore, not alone. When the individual presents a portion of past Christian history and proclaims good news for the present, the Spirit connects the word from the past with the perceptions of the present.

The Spirit is thus active when an effective speaker helps us make the connection between what we call to memory and what we are groping to know. With the Spirit's assistance, the speaker presents images of human reality that could encourage the incarnation of a new world, for an image can create an emotional or whole connection between word and hearer. The event of communication happens between speaker and hearer. By recreating or enacting a text—not translating it but identifying the event of the text and mediating it toward the present—the Spirit enables the sermon to happen between the pew and pulpit, not in the latter alone. The sermon is shared understanding and a new horizon.

In Christian conversation of all types we risk ourselves and our horizon of understanding to the communicative process as we participate with each other in the Spirit's creation of a world. That world, in turn, touches those who would reveal its truth; we are "played" by it. We cannot control the game or its outcome for there is no model or method for playing this game, only vulnerability. Being is relational.

The danger inherent in using words or images to talk "about" God is that the word or image itself becomes an idol.

Theologians would be the first to admit we can never know all there is to know about God. However, their interpretive vocabulary would be improved if they placed less emphasis on talking "about" God and more on "revealing" God. The danger inherent in using words or images to talk "about" God is that the word or image itself becomes an idol. God is greater than any of our words or images. We would do well to remember "the inevitable distance between our words and the divine reality [and like] the mystics . . . not [be] inclined to identify our words with God."[133]

How, then shall we speak on controversial issues? By surrendering ourselves to the discovery of new being. By maintaining dialogue. By speaking with conviction and compassion while at the same time we listen and learn.

Parker J. Palmer in *To Know as We are Known/A Spirituality of Education* writes, "Learning the truth requires that we enter into personal relationship with what the words reveal. To know truth we must follow it with our lives."[134] To remain true to its message, speaking must be "an event, an alive, moving, and changing occurrence . . . ."[135] Thus, each communicative event must emerge anew, addressing the happenings of our daily lives where the invisible is made incarnate.

Implications for the Contemporary Debate

Speaker, hearer, and Spirit participate in revelatory speaking, and meaning happens. This understanding of the communicative process has implications for our conversations on sexuality, or any issue of controversy.

There are, for example, important implications for biblical preaching. Preachers frequently bypass serious discussion of what Scripture has to say on difficult issues. Perhaps they have not thought out their own positions on the subject. They may suspect that calling attention to a particular biblical injunction will offend specific members of the congregation, often those who seem already to have more than their share of difficulties. Another reason for avoiding Scripture passages that relate to controversial issues is that a preacher may fear that a discussion of biblical material may uncover or create divisions within the congregation.

In such circumstances, the preacher is tempted to omit talking about the Bible. The preacher may hope that the issue will somehow "solve itself" or may believe that other fields of study—medicine or social sciences, for example—provide a more effective means of reaching a conclusion. To remain silent about what the Bible says, however, would be a major mistake. The clash of expectations and attitudes that the preacher would avoid is precisely the arena in which the Spirit is active. Here the Good News of Jesus Christ is most likely to be heard.

Had Jesus' offensive words to the rich man not been read and preached, there would have been no Franciscans or other mendicant orders. Were it not for wrestling with the Psalms and Romans, there might not have been a Lutheran reformation in the sixteenth century or a Methodist revival in the eighteenth. If we do not allow ourselves to struggle with the uncomfortable words of the Pentateuch or Paul on sexuality, we may shut ourselves off from the renewing power of the Spirit.

CHAPTER

7

Christian mental health professionals are frequently asked to comment on the issue of homosexuality and the church. Yet few are up-to-date on the current research concerning the questions they are asked. This chapter explores four basic questions which the church might ask the Christian psychologist. We'll discuss the best answers to those questions available from the behavioral science literature. These questions are: (a) Is homosexuality an intrinsically psychopathological condition? (b) Is an individual's homosexual orientation caused by factors beyond his or her voluntary control? (c) Is change to heterosexuality impossible for the homosexual? and (d) Is the expression of erotic sexuality essential to psychological wholeness?

Homosexuality: The Behavioral Sciences and the Church[136]

Stanton L. Jones and Donald E. Workman

Christian psychologists should be careful when attempting to articulate "consensus views" on these questions. Our current knowledge about homosexuality is much more rudimentary than is usually acknowledged. Science, then, may have less proper impact on the ethical deliberations of the church than most people think.

Today the church is grappling with the moral status of homosexual behavior and homoerotic orientation, and hence with its pastoral response to homosexual persons. Denominations and other Christian groups are rightly asking the behavioral sciences for insights of relevance to these discussions.

We presuppose that the sciences, a potent force in contemporary culture, can and should influence the thought life of the Christian church. The church has always readily interacted with academic culture when it was healthy, drawing from and dialoguing with it in many areas including the humanities (especially philosophy) and the sciences. This dialogue has hopefully added depth and relevance to the theology and ethics of the church without obscuring or undermining its distinctive faith story.

The church's decisions should reflect an accurate knowledge about what the social sciences can legitimately say on this topic without allowing its response . . . to be dictated by the social sciences.

In avoiding the error of completely rejecting dialogue with culture, however, the church must not over-identify with cultural influences or take its agenda from those influences.[137]

Holifield has documented the tendency for the church, in times of doubt about its historic identity, to allow its mission and identity to be defined by psychological concepts and the broader influences of secular culture rather than by its own distinctive tradition.[138]

The church is being urged from many fronts to alter its historic positions on the issue of homosexuality. This chapter argues that the church's decisions should reflect an accurate knowledge about what the social sciences can legitimately say on this topic without allowing its response on this or any matter to be dictated by the social sciences.

The church might appropriately ask many questions of the social sciences. This chapter focuses upon four questions important to the church's decision making on this topic. First, is homosexuality psychopathological? Positions for or against the status of homosexuality as psychopathology are regularly offered in connection with the response of the church to homosexual persons and behaviors. Second, is homosexual orientation caused by factors beyond a person's voluntary control? This question is raised because positions regarding moral accountability for homosexual acts and/or orientation, as well as ideas about change processes, are based on models of causation. Third, is change to heterosexuality impossible for homosexuals? Again, moral accountability usually presumes the individual could act otherwise, and pastoral direction must be informed by the best evidence regarding the possibility of change. Finally, we ask, is the overt expression of erotic sexuality essential to psychological wholeness? The answer to this question should help pastors make judgments regarding the benefits of various forms of guidance. This chapter will review the data relevant to these questions and conclude with an interpretive summary of these matters.

By "homosexual behavior" we refer to acts between two persons of the same sex that engender sexual arousal (usually to the point of orgasm). By "homosexual orientation" or "homosexuality" we refer to a stable erotic and/or affectional preference for persons of the same sex. Persons can engage in homosexual behavior without being homosexual; others can have a homosexual orientation without ever engaging in overt homosexual behavior. Since preference and orientation are loose concepts and human experience is quite diverse, many persons and acts cannot be easily classified by any descriptive system, including this one.

Is Homosexuality a Psychopathology?

The most simplistic answer to this question is "Of course not!" Since the American Psychiatric Association (APA) removed homosexuality from its approved list of pathological psychiatric conditions in 1974, homosexuality is no longer considered psychopathological. Before we accept such an answer, we need to understand a little of the history and context behind the APA's action.

First, while the deletion of homosexuality from the DSM (the APA's Diagnostic and Statistical Manual) was in response to a majority vote of the APA, it appears that the majority of the APA membership viewed homosexuality as pathological in spite of the vote. Four years after the vote, a survey found that 69% of psychiatrists believed that homosexuality "usually represents a pathological adaptation."[139] The editor of the journal that published this survey suggested that the 1974 vote "might have been affected by socio-political considerations."[140] The vote may have demonstrated support for homosexual civil rights and not the views of psychiatrists about the pathological status of homosexuality.

Second, the vote was called at a time of tremendous social upheaval and change. The volatility of the social order may itself have inappropriately influenced the decision process.

Third, the vote was taken under conditions of explicit threats from the gay rights establishment to continue disruptive demonstrations which would impede APA conventions and research.

Finally, the action was taken with unconventional speed that circumvented the channels normally used to consider issues.[141]

The removal of homosexuality from the DSM does not and cannot conclusively decide the issue of the pathological status of homosexuality. We are still left asking the question: "Is homosexuality abnormal?" While there is no absolute standard for judging normality or abnormality, four empirical criteria are often used to define behavioral patterns as abnormal. These are:

1. statistical infrequency
2. personal distress
3. maladaptiveness
4. deviation from social norms.

Is Homosexuality Statistically Infrequent?

As a life-long exclusive or near-exclusive orientation, homosexuality is not a common pattern, but neither is it rare. Bieber suggested that 1-2% of the adult male population are exclusively or near-exclusively homosexual, while Hunt put the figure at 2.3%.[142] Kinsey, Pomeroy, and Martin found 4% of white males to be exclusively homosexual throughout life after adolescence and a total of 10% of white males to be mostly or exclusively homosexual during at least a three-year period between the ages of 16 and 55.[143] The incidence of female homosexuality, on which less research exists, is commonly reported to be less than that for males.

The studies by Kinsey, Pomeroy, and Martin cannot be interpreted as saying that 1 out of 10 persons in the general population is homosexual (a common assertion).[144] From their data, we would expect a cross-section of the population at any point in time to show up to 4% of lifetime homosexual males to be actively pursuing their homosexual orientation, and some fraction of the "mostly or exclusively homosexual for at least 3 years" group to be engaged in homosexual practices. Combining these findings with the lower incidence of homosexuality among women, and remembering that the researchers' sampling over-represented persons with homosexual experience (for example, prison inmates), we would expect that an estimate from a general population of both sexes would find much less than 10% exclusive homosexual preference at any point in time.

> *... we would expect that an estimate from a general population of both sexes would find much less than 10% exclusive homosexual preference at any point in time.*

One of the major surprises of the Kinsey, Pomeroy, and Martin studies was not the frequency of exclusive homosexuality, but the fact that the incidence rate for at least a one-time occurrence was much higher than societal abhorrence would have suggested. The findings that "*37 percent* of the total male population has *at least some overt homosexual experience* to the point of orgasm between adolescence and old age" was something the authors "were totally unprepared to find . . . when this research was originally undertaken."[145] As we have noted, however, their data are generally believed to over-represent male homosexuality due to sampling biases in their research. Pomeroy, one of Kinsey's coauthors, has said that "the magic 37 percent . . . was, no doubt, overestimated."[146] William Simon, formerly a research associate at the Kinsey Institute, suggested that only "2 to 3 percent of the male population has a serious, long-term homosexual pattern. Another 7 or 8 percent have casual or episodic homosexual experience."[147]

Even with a lower estimate of incidence than public perception might indicate, we will have no absolute cutting score for judging pathology by statistical infrequency. No one has been or will be able to define pathology or health using only population norms and statistical frequency. Choosing a cut-off point is inherently arbitrary.

Does Homosexuality Always and Inherently Involve Personal Distress?

Contemporary research has shown that homosexuals as a group are not more emotionally disturbed, according to current standards, than heterosexuals.[148] Bell and Weinberg did document higher rates of depression and loneliness, as well as "more paranoia and psychosomatic symptoms" among their homosexual sample.[149] They also found that 18% of white homosexual males reported attempting suicide at least once, compared to 3% of heterosexual respondents. Additionally, Kus documented elevated substance abuse rates in this population.[150] It seems that some behaviors indicative of distress are more common among homosexuals in these studies. While there are studies which have demonstrated a correlation between homosexuality and neurotic behavior, it cannot be generally concluded that remarkable levels of personal distress are a consistent part of homosexual experience.[151] Most homosexuals in the Bell and Weinburg study (which was not a random sample) did not regret being homosexual and were not judged to exhibit psychopathological symptoms.

It is common for many researchers and writers in this area to attribute elevated levels of distress among homosexuals (such as depression or suicidality) not to discomfort produced by the orientation itself, but rather to the interaction of homosexuals with a rejecting and punitive society. They liken these responses to those of any persecuted or rejected minority. While this explanation is typically a *post hoc* interpretation of research, there is an important point here: Few heterosexuals know the stress of living under persecution for their erotic feelings. Social hostility toward homosexuals is therefore bound to influence any comparative measure of emotional stability.

Is Homosexuality Maladaptive?

This can be answered with reference to a number of standards. Focusing on the least controversial dimensions of "personal harm," we come up with a mixed report.

Positively, homosexuals have been prominent among those who have contributed to our society and culture: artists, scientists, literary figures, educators, and so forth. Homosexuality itself does not seem to prevent a person from being a productive and functional member of society. We note, however, that this is an argument by association. One could argue against homosexuality by associating it instead with perverse acts committed by specific homosexual individuals. Clearly, neither argument provides any useful information about adaptiveness.

On another level, the biological adaptiveness of homosexuality has been questioned. Scientists have suggested that homosexual behavior does not contribute to the propagation of the species and hence is abnormal. This view is not often voiced today, as sociobiologists now suggest that under some circumstances (such as overpopulation) homosexuality can contribute to overall species enhancement by preventing a subpopulation from contributing to further propagation.

On the other hand, the AIDS epidemic has given pause to many regarding the biological adaptiveness of male homosexuality. The rampant spread of AIDS in the male homosexual population appears to be due to many factors, including several that are endemic to male homosexuality itself. First, anal intercourse almost always involves tearing of rectal tissue, resulting in semen-blood contact (the two fluids containing the highest concentration of the AIDS virus in the body). Second, promiscuity among many homosexuals promoted a rapid spread of the virus. Third, some aspects of the stressful gay life-style may undermine the body's normal capacity for fighting off infection (including the AIDS virus).

Homosexuality itself does not seem to prevent a person from being a productive and functional member of society.

Another area of controversy concerning the adaptiveness of homosexuality involves relational stability. Here the crux of the matter is again the question of definition. While it appears that lesbians are able to form long-term relationships in a manner comparable to that of heterosexuals, male homosexuals as a population show a greatly reduced capacity for such relationships and a clear propensity for promiscuous practices. Bell and Weinberg found in a nonrandom but large sample that only 10% of male homosexual respondents could be classified as existing in "close couple" relationships, and that these relationships could only be characterized as "relatively monogamous" or "relatively less promiscuous."[152] In the same study, 28% of white homosexual males reported having had 1,000 or more homosexual partners at the time they were interviewed, while only

17% reported having had fewer than 50 homosexual partners (thus, 83% of white homosexual males had had sexual relations with 50 or more partners in their lifetimes). In addition, 79% of white homosexual males reported that more than half of their sexual partners were strangers.[153]

Fidelity to and stability within a monogamous relationship used to be a prominent feature in definitions of emotional health, but it is rarely emphasized today.[154] If one presupposes that the capacity to form stable monogamous erotic relationships is an essential adaptive capacity, then real difficulties for male homosexuals emerge. If the psychological community deemphasizes relational stability among its criteria of adaptiveness or healthy emotional adjustment, then promiscuity in the male homosexual community does not constitute maladjustment.

Finally, we would judge the adaptiveness of homosexuality by whether or not homosexuals achieve what we understand to be wholeness and health. That is, we could judge adaptiveness by our model or theory of normal human development. It is on this basis that conventional psychoanalytically oriented practitioners continue to judge homosexuality as representing a fixation or regression in development.[155] Heterosexuality is presumed to be the natural endpoint of growth for individuals in the traditional psychoanalytic model; homosexuals do not reach that endpoint and therefore their condition is judged maladaptive. However, developmental models are always open to dispute—which is why the psychological and psychiatric communities have collectively retreated from using such models to formally judge normalcy.

Does Homosexuality Violate Societal Norms?

Unquestionably, homosexuality violates American societal norms. Recent studies of public opinion show that 73% of the general public views all instances of homosexual behavior as immoral.[156] The majority of Americans are exclusively heterosexual, and there is unquestionably a strong social stigma attached to being homosexual within a predominantly heterosexual culture.

In a recent study, Nevid documented increased levels of negative affect (anxiety and hostility) in heterosexual subjects when exposed to homoerotic stimuli.[157] Interestingly, rather than discussing potential negative implications for the homosexual community, he concluded by talking about the defensive role negative affect plays in heterosexuals' denial of their "homosexual tendencies."[158]

In the case of homosexuality, instead of reflecting the majority view, the mental health establishment seems to have committed itself to revising the predominant public response—to normalizing behavior which is clearly rejected by the public. This stance is especially puzzling in light of the recent national survey of mental health professionals conducted by Allen Bergin.[159] Bergin reported that 57% of surveyed mental health professionals agreed or strongly agreed with the statement that having "preference for a heterosexual sex relationship" was an important criterion for mental health.[160]

Conclusions on Homosexuality as Psychopathology

Determining whether or not homosexuality is inherently pathological is a difficult and unresolved task. Homosexuality is infrequent in the larger society, but without an absolute cutoff point, this empirical finding is not decisive. The empirical evidence is also inconclusive regarding whether homosexuality is itself strongly linked with personal distress, though the weight of evidence suggests it is not. The arguments regarding maladaptiveness are also inconclusive given the varying standards by which we might judge maladaptativeness. Finally, it is clear that homosexuality violates societal norms. This is a mixed scorecard, reflecting the confusion and disagreement in the field today about the pathological status of homosexuality.

Is a Homosexual Orientation Caused by Factors Beyond a Person's Voluntary Control?

This question plumbs the troubled depths of research into causes of homosexuality. Among the factors complicating this research is the diversity of persons to whom the description "homosexual" applies. The major causes of homosexual orientation that have been proposed include genetic, prenatal hormonal, postnatal hormonal, and psychological factors. Following is a brief summary of the evidence for each of these.

Genetic Factors

Early research into the causes of homosexuality suggested a strong genetic component in causation. A study by F. Kallman showed

100% concordance for homosexuality in monozygotic twins.[161] These results have not been duplicated (Kallman himself later called them a "statistical artifact"), though it is generally concluded that there is probably some degree of genetic influence in the development of a homosexual orientation for some persons.[162]

John Money recently concluded that "according to the currently available evidence, the sex chromosomes do not directly determine or program psychosexual status as heterosexual, bisexual, or homosexual."[163] In other words, research showing greater concordance for homosexuality in monozygotic twins as opposed to dizygotic twins or other siblings can be explained, in Money's opinion, by psychosexual influences possibly interacting with prenatal hormonal factors.

Prenatal Hormonal Factors

Studies introducing abnormal hormone levels into animal fetuses have shown that prenatal hormones do affect sexual differentiation and erotic development in animals. The right dose of sex hormones given to an animal fetus at a critical time can result in that animal showing sexually inverted behavior when mature, including homosexual erotic preferences. These effects are complex and multifaceted.

Hormone levels in the human fetus can radically affect the physical development, brain functioning, gender orientation, and adult behavior of the person. In humans, for example, fluctuations in hormone levels induced by drugs ingested by the mother during periods of fetal development have resulted in various forms of hermaphroditism and pseudohermaphroditism, with their concomitant disruptions of physical and psychosocial development.[164]

Does this research suggest a prenatal hormonal cause of homosexuality? There are theorists who propose such a model. Ellis and Ames have proposed that human sexual orientation is largely determined between the second and fifth month of gestation due to fetal exposure to testosterone, its primary metabolite estriadol, and other sex hormones.[165] Their theory is challenging, and they surveyed an impressive array of research to support their ideas, the majority of which come from laboratory animal studies.

Their logic, however, is debatable. Their argument is that (a) it is possible to produce sex inversions, including homosexual erotic preferences, by prenatal hormonal manipulations in *animals*, (b) there is no conclusive evidence showing that postnatal hormonal or psychosocial factors cause *human* homosexual orientation, and (c) human epidemiological studies of the incidence of homosexuality are not incompatible with their theory. All this has lead them to conclude that *human* erotic inversion is prenatally determined.

While their conclusions are thought-provoking, they are not compelling. Two implications of their theory are worth specific mention. In the majority of the animal research they survey, the development of homosexual orientation in the studied animals is precipitated by highly abnormal variations in maternal hormonal levels, and is usually associated with other indisputable alterations in gender-typical behavioral patterns. Their view suggests that if homosexual orientation is a response to an abnormal maternal hormonal environment, then homosexuality is abnormal in itself (a "birth defect" of sorts?). They recognized this implication at some level, as they closed their article with a caution for those who might use their theory to argue for attempts at prevention of homosexuality. They stated that societal tolerance of homosexuals is "in tune with the evidence reviewed."[166] They were unclear as to why they frown upon research in prevention.

Ellis and Ames' theory would link homosexual object preference with other gender "inversions," clearly distinguishing homosexual persons from the rest of their gender group.

Secondly, it is worth noting that, in the past, one defense of the essential normalcy of the homosexual has been the assertion that erotic preference is the only difference between the homosexual and the rest of the population. Ellis and Ames' theory would link homosexual object preference with other gender "inversions," clearly distinguishing homosexual persons from the rest of their gender group.

In contrast to Ellis and Ames' ideas, John Money has concluded quite explicitly: "there is no human evidence that prenatal hormonalization alone, independently of postnatal history, inexorably preordains [homosexuality]. Rather, neonatal antecedents may facilitate a homosexual . . . orientation, provided the postnatal determinants in the social and communicational history are also facilitative."[167] In other words, prenatal influences may provide a push in the direction of homosexuality, but there is no conclusive evidence that this push is powerful enough to be considered determinative, or that this push is present for all homosexuals. Money also says that postnatal (psychological) influences may result in a homosexual orientation even in the absence of any predisposing prenatal influences.

> *There is no clear basis for the suggestion that homosexual orientation is completely determined before birth . . .*

Money's conclusions were more broadly based on the findings in the field than those of Ellis and Ames, who essentially dismissed psychosocial research on the origin of homosexuality. It seems reasonable that prenatal hormonal influences may facilitate or contribute to homosexual orientation in some individuals, but those influences cannot be considered operative in all homosexuals and cannot be considered to be determinative. There is no clear basis for the suggestion that homosexual orientation is completely determined before birth through genetic or hormonal channels, though prenatal hormonal factors may be part of the causal pattern for some individuals.

Postnatal Hormonal Factors
There have been a variety of intriguing and contradictory findings in this area, and many failures to replicate earlier dramatic findings. The general consensus has been that there are no major hormonal or physiological differences between heterosexuals and homosexuals.[168] In any case, the literature consistently concludes that nonextreme hormone level variations have little impact on sexual interests and choices in humans. Human beings are so complex and so responsive to their social world that there is very little purely biologic determination of their behavior and preferences.

Psychological Factors
Psychoanalytic theory. According to Bieber, "In every case I have examined, studied, or treated, homosexuality was the consequence of

serious disturbances during childhood development."[169] Bieber has worked exclusively with male homosexuals in therapy, so his is not a random sample of the homosexual population and his findings are limited to male homosexuals.

Homosexuality, according to Bieber, is due primarily to a profound disturbance in parent-child relationships. A boy may have a father who is distant, cold, unavailable, or rejecting, and a mother who is overly warm, smothering, and controlling. As a result of his father's rejection, the boy's desire to identify with the father is frustrated, planting the seeds of both fear and longing for closeness to a male. The smothering relationship with the mother further increases the likelihood that the boy will not establish a complete male identity. Bieber and others have thus argued that a boy growing up in such an environment avoids heterosexual activities due to fear of the aggressiveness of other males with whom he is competing. At the same time, the boy is attracted by other men because of his longing for closeness to another male.

Some evidence exists that similar dynamics are present for lesbians as well, where the major disturbance seems to be in the relationship with the mother. Lesbians report greater than expected frequencies of rejecting and negative relationships with their mothers.[170]

Bieber's theory is based on clinical work and research with nearly 1,000 homosexuals. His research meets with varying responses in the mental health community, ranging from outright dismissal to total acceptance. Judd Marmor seems accurate when he says that "boys exposed to this kind of family background have a greater than average likelihood of becoming homosexual." In other words, this background probably facilitates development of the homosexual orientation, but does not determine it and is not the only causal factor.[171] Socarides and many others offer different psychoanalytic interpretations of homosexuality.[172] Friedman makes the balanced judgment that psychoanalytic scholars have not offered compelling evidence for their theories, but do have something to offer in the understanding of the phenomenon.[173]

Learning theories. Behavioral hypotheses regarding the development of homosexuality suggest that early erotic and other learning experiences shape erotic orientation. For example, a boy with troubled family relationships and a preexisting tendency toward effeminate behavior may experience his early erotic experiences in a homosexual fashion.[174] These experiences provide the basis on which subsequent experiences are pursued. A child who is homosexually seduced may use that experience as the basis for subsequent sexual fantasy and dreaming. By beginning to define himself as homosexual, he may selectively choose subsequent homosexual interactions even when heterosexual options are available.

Storms, for instance, has argued that erotic orientation is typically solidified during adolescence through the interaction of sex drive (a biological factor) and experience.[175] In normal social development, boys turn from exclusively same-sex friendships to mixed gender friendships around the time of puberty. This aids the development of heterosexuality, since boys have greater exposure to girls at about the same time their sex drive begins to blossom in response to the pubescent surge of sex hormones. For some boys, however, precocious onset of sex drive begins quite early, when they are still predominantly in same-sex relationships. Since at onset the sex drive is undirected, early onset of sex drive can lead to direction of sexual urges at other boys since this is who the child is around.

Storms cited data supporting his theory such as the greater incidences of homosexuality in populations where early sex drive onset occurs, such as pubescent athletes. Storms also argued that lesbianism has a lower incidence than male homosexuality because girls experience later onset of sex drive than boys even though they tend to go through puberty earlier. Storms' theory is a recent one which has not yet been widely critiqued.

Other psychological factors. Two bodies of evidence suggest that the causation of homosexuality is neither exclusively genetic nor biological. First, homosexual behavior occurs often in the animal kingdom. Denniston concluded from his review of research in this area that homosexual behavior "occurs in every type of animal that has been carefully studied . . . it has little relation to hormonal or structural abnormality. . . . It is behavioral conditioning that is directive, with hormones playing a permissive or generalized activating role."[176] In other words, hormones don't force the behavior, but experiences of homosexual pleasure or social conditioning do play a role. It further seems that most homosexual behavior in the animal kingdom occurs in the context of interaction between dominant and subordinate animals, under conditions of unavailability of other-sex sexual partners, or under such stressors as crowding. While homosexual behavior in animals is not uncommon, stable, lifelong homosexual orientation is quite unusual, though not unknown.[177]

Second, homosexual behavior occurs to some extent in all known human cultures, but the form it takes varies from culture to culture. This suggests that the culture's view of homosexual behavior is a prominent influence upon the behavior itself. One important point to draw from this research is that while homosexual behavior seems to exist in all societies, the concept of homosexual orientation as a lifelong and stable pattern does not, and is rare in preindustrial societies.[178]

While homosexual behavior seems to exist in all societies, the concept of homosexual orientation as a lifelong and stable pattern does not, and is rare in preindustrial societies.

Many cultures have a prescribed place for homosexual behavior, and the cultural view seems to channel human experience. For example, Stoller and Herdt describe the practices of the Sambia tribe of New Guinea, where all males are taken from their families around the age of seven to live communally with the older single men of the tribe.[179] In that company, prepubertal boys are expected to perform oral sex on the postpubertal single men, as they believe that boys can only grow to be men when fed on the "milk of men." When the boys reach puberty, they switch roles to be the ones on whom oral sex is performed. Finally, when they reach marrying age, they are expected to take wives and function exclusively as heterosexual married men. The Sambia males achieve this switch almost without exception, a striking change given the extent of juvenile homosexual experience.

Carrier has summarized many cross-cultural studies by saying that homosexual behavior seems to occur for two main reasons: either lack of available other-sex partners or as part of a culturally defined ritual.[180] Neither of these causes can be invoked for understanding homosexual orientation in our society, but it does seem clear that the view of behavior embraced by a society shapes subsequent behavior. This is one reason why the decisions of the church on this matter are important; these decisions participate in the shaping of our culture.

Conclusions on Causation

There is a general if informal consensus today that no theory of homosexuality can explain such a diverse phenomenon. It certainly seems that there is no completely determinative genetic, hormonal or psychological cause of homosexual orientation. Rather, there appear to be a variety of facilitating influences which provide a push in the direction of homosexuality for some persons. The personal influences (psychological, familial, and cultural) seem to be most important. We concur with the conclusion of John Money that while homosexuality can develop without genetic or hormonal factors being operative, it generally does not develop without the influence of learning and socialization.[181]

Is Change to Heterosexuality Impossible for the Homosexual?

We are disturbed by the popular idea that change is impossible for the homosexual. The evidence here is clear. First, change is possible for some. Bieber, for example, reported a 33% success rate for conversion to heterosexuality.[182] Masters and Johnson reported a 50-60% cure or improvement rate for highly motivated clients.[183] Socarides reported a success rate in achieving full heterosexual functioning of almost 50%.[184] Perhaps these modest success rates were obtained from unusually committed clients, but, curiously, opponents of such therapies often use the statistics about modest cure rates to argue that no cure is possible. Every study of conversion therapy in literature reports some successes.

Second, change is difficult. No study suggests that change comes from willingness to change or some simple set of procedures. The consensus seems to be that change is most likely when motivation is strong, when there is a history of successful heterosexual functioning, when gender identity issues are not present, and when involvement in actual homosexual practice has been minimal. Change of homosexual orientation may well be impossible for some by any natural means.

Third, a number of Christian groups (such as Evangelicals Concerned) claim change is impossible or *highly* unlikely. These organizations urge Christians to accept homosexuality. But a growing number of Christian ministries are attempting to help homosexuals change. Many of these groups are represented by the umbrella organization Exodus International and/or use the methods of Homosexuals Anonymous.[185]

These groups offer a variety of approaches, but generally agree that change is a difficult and painful process of renouncing sinful practices and attitudes and reaching out to grasp the promise of God's help. They suggest that struggling with homosexual attraction is a lifelong task, but that the person who enters that struggle can expect gradual change. Unfortunately, these groups have not systematically studied their success rates. The Pattison and Pattison study is one of the few which documents change through purely "spiritual" means, but it does not document success rates—only that some success is possible through such means.[186]

Is Expression of Erotic Sexuality Essential to Wholeness?

This complex issue can be considered many ways. Are those who advise homosexuals to change to heterosexuality, or, if this is not possible, avoid physical expression of their erotic urges for the rest of their lives, interfering with human wholeness? Obviously the homosexual person is being asked to do something that is not easy. Most heterosexuals would not relish abstinence, either.

Psychology has no uniform answer to this question. In looking for solutions one confronts a babel of voices, each crying out a different answer. Our sexually charged society claims that sexual gratification is somehow fundamental to human happiness.

> *Our sexually charged society claims that sexual gratification is somehow fundamental to human happiness.*

Unfortunately, there is no empirical research directly bearing on this question. In fact, each of the major personality theories puts sexuality in a different place in the life of a person. Some place it in the core of a person (psychoanalytic theory) and others put it on the periphery (social cognitive theory). However, none of the major theories in academic psychology assert that the expression of genital erotic urges is essential to human well-being.

Conclusion

The behavioral sciences do not hold the answers to church deliberations about the morality of homosexual behavior, the ordination of homosexual persons, and other related questions. But the church can learn much about homosexuality from the behavioral sciences. Let us summarize this chapter's major implications.

Is Homosexuality a Psychopathology?

As psychologists, we are committed to a minimalist and conservative criteria for defining psychopathology in the same sense as schizophrenia, depression, or phobic disorders. But as Christians, we believe that genital homosexual acts are immoral, and that immorality is an abnormal (unintended by God) condition for humanity.[187] Further, we feel that a Christian understanding of persons commits one to regarding heterosexuality as the optimal goal of human sexual and affective fulfillment, much in the way we described earlier in discussing models of optimal personal development. Therefore, homosexuality must be regarded as a problematic erotic orientation which contemporary social science can help to understand and hopefully to change.

As Christians, we believe that genital homosexual acts are immoral, and that immorality is an abnormal (unintended by God) condition for humanity.

Rather than regarding homosexuality as a pathology, it may be helpful to develop an alternative designation such as "developmental abnormality."[188] Such a move must not, however, be used to assert that homosexual individuals are disordered in all aspects of their being. Many homosexuals are loving, creative, compassionate people of great wisdom and insight.

This leads us, for example, to support the ordination of celibate persons of homosexual orientation who are otherwise suited and called to the ministry.

Is Homosexuality Developed Involuntarily?
It appears that the diverse range of human dispositions that might be labeled homosexual result from a host of factors. Causal patterns unquestionably vary from person to person. The scientific literature often seems to imply that the human being is passively buffeted about by external influences. This view seems subChristian, but a Christian view of persons is certainly not committed to denying that external factors do operate to influence or shape a person's life. Perhaps the Christian view would suggest that we respond to external influences with small or large responsible acts of our own, thus adding *our own choices* to the host of causal factors that shape our personalities. We often fail to see the impact of our choices because many times it is not the grand climactic decisions that shape our lives, but the small cumulative ones. These everyday choices result in our being kind or cruel, envious or affirming, idolatrous or godly.

Perhaps for many the process of becoming a homosexual involves a host of deceptively small decisions which interact with influences over which we have no control, with the final result being homosexual orientation. We cannot, on the basis of scientific evidence, rule out at least partial human accountability for our sexual orientations any more than we can give up our responsibility for helping to create other problems in living.

We point out that genetic and hormonal explanations of homosexuality at most indicate that these factors facilitate or allow the development of homosexuality. Psychological theories do not prove and do not uniformly suggest that homosexual preference is determined in early childhood—though this is the majority opinion. The learning explanation obviously focuses on sexual experiences around and after puberty, and the psychoanalytic model, usually associated with early childhood causes, leaves open the possibility that later influences could have a significant impact. Psychoanalyst Robert Friedman concluded that "the final sexual orientation may not consolidate until after puberty."[189] If consolidation of sexual orientation does not occur until after puberty for some, then partial human responsibility is a possible factor in some cases.[190]

Perhaps, on the other hand, some persons *are* the helpless victims of powerful influences (hormonal, familial) which shape their orientation in its original form. God unquestionably allows some of his children to bear the heavy consequences of events for which they are not responsible (for example, the person who becomes quadriplegic in a church bus accident).

> *God unquestionably allows some of his children to bear the heavy consequences of events for which they are not responsible . . .*

Beyond sorting through one's "life story," establishing responsibility for sexual orientation may have little relevance for the homosexual adult (except that knowledge of how this orientation developed could help guide treatment efforts, pastoral counseling, and possible prevention and education efforts with families). Establishing partial responsibility for the adult state may not assist change efforts in any way. Some conditions for which we are partially responsible may be irreversible once fully developed (for example, a person's decision to begin using drugs may lead to irreversible effects including lifelong craving and danger of relapse).

Even if it were to be proven conclusively that homosexual orientation develops due to factors totally beyond the individual's control, we would still need to debate moral guidelines and responsibility for acting upon that preference. In other words, we would still need to differentiate between responsibility for homosexual orientation versus responsibility for homosexual acts. By analogy, an adult child of an alcoholic *may* have a biological predisposition to respond positively to alcohol intake, but must face the responsibility of choosing whether or not to indulge that predisposition. Certainly homosexuals who are addicted to compulsive sexual acting-out are manifesting diminished responsibility and should be assisted in redeveloping control. But noncompulsive homosexuals must be seen as responsible for the specific acts they commit.

To further support this position, we note that genetic and environmental influences have causal roles in forming both heterosexual and homosexual erotic orientation. It follows then that the ethics of sexual behavior applies similarly to both. To say that persons cannot be held responsible for their sexual acts because of environmental or genetic influences would release both homosexuals and heterosexuals from responsible adherence to scriptural mandates. The Bible treats homosexual and heterosexual misconduct similarly by prescribing the same sentence within Hebrew culture to each. Therefore, it is unjustifiable to dismiss moral accountability for homosexual acts simply because such acts are based on determinative factors, since comparable factors which are also beyond an individual's control influence heterosexual misconduct.

Is Change Possible?

Change to heterosexuality is certainly possible for some, but the success rates are modest at best. If the Christian church judges homosexual behavior to be nonproblematic on ethical grounds, pastors would be ill-advised to urge change efforts on the homosexual. If the behavior is deemed immoral, then change efforts are warranted in spite of the difficulty of such pursuits.

If change does not occur, is it contrary to the well-being of the person to commend abstinence? Neither behavioral science nor Christian theology suggest that abstinence is detrimental to human welfare, or that expression of genital eroticism is necessary for wholeness. Genital expression was and is intended to occur within marriage, and many of us never have the opportunity, or forgo the opportunity, for overt interpersonal sexual gratification (for example, Jesus). It seems inconceivable that God would create us with a drive that *must* be expressed for wholeness and at the same time put up a wall stifling its expression. Surely our sexuality is central to our personhood, but is it a force in our lives which must be genitally expressed for us to be whole? We find this idea unacceptable.

Christian Faith and the Issue of Homosexuality

One issue that is foundational here is our understanding of the Christian faith. A vision of the faith that emphasizes salvation asserts that though we are good in many ways there is something wrong with us. This view assumes that our faith will involve diagnosing that which is faulty in us (sin), and will prescribe ways to mend the flaws (redemption). In the process, we will be called to become that which we are not (sanctification)—to act *against* our natures.

On the other hand, a vision of faith that emphasizes self-realization would emphasize our naturally positive tendencies and seek to enhance them. This view of faith would emphasize affirmation rather than repentance, growth rather than change, and enhancement rather than sacrifice.

We have embraced a position that gives priority to the former view without denying the latter. We mention this because it is important to decide

a. whether the diagnosis of defect and fault (sin) rightly requires change even if this might involve discomfort or suffering

b. whether this is rightly expected of redeemed human persons according to our Christian view of life.

Ultimately, we will make these decisions based on our understanding and experience of Christian faith and the life of the church. The findings of the behavioral sciences will not dictate the stance of the church toward homosexual persons and actions.

Homosexual and heterosexual persons are created in the image of God, and for this reason deserve the greatest love, wisdom, and fairness which the earthly church is capable of giving. As St. Paul teaches us, love is kind and not self-righteous. It is not easily angered and does not delight in evil, but rejoices with the truth (1 Corinthians 13). In this context, we have tried to clarify the insights which the behavioral sciences can offer to the church in its theological, ethical, and pastoral deliberations about Christian persons and their sexual orientations and behaviors.

CHAPTER

8

The 1991 "*Blue Book* Report" of the Human Affairs Commission recommended both the preparation of liturgies to celebrate same-sex unions and the ordination of sexually active gays and lesbians. Providing little support for these suggestions, the Report even admitted that it did not sufficiently relate its recommendations to Christian

Traditional Sexual Ethics: Making a Case

David A. Scott

Scripture and tradition. The Report's recommendations certainly do collide with traditional Christian teaching on human sexuality.

The Report, therefore, left bishops and deputies with two problems. First, they needed to learn from other sources about traditional Christian sexual ethics and reasons why the church should teach them today. Second, the bishops and deputies were left to support or reject the recommendations without sufficient knowledge about the rationale for doing so, or even the full content of the alternative sexual ethic that underlay the Report's recommendations.

This chapter responds to these two problems. It will summarize the key teachings of the traditional Christian sexual ethic, identifying some of its roots and bases. It will then summarize the alternative ethic, which approves any sexual relationship that manifests justice and respect, whether between homosexual or heterosexual, married or unmarried partners. This chapter will clarify the cultural background of this alternative ethic and raise critical questions. The main purpose is to advocate a creative retrieval of traditional Christian sexual norms.

The Traditional Christian Sexual Morality

The traditional Christian sexual norms can be summarized under three points:

1. Full genital-sexual relations should occur between a man and a woman; in other words, they should be heterosexual.

2. Full sexual intimacy should be reserved for the bond and covenant of a lifelong, sexually exclusive marriage.

3. The ends or purposes of sexual intercourse include in principle (allowing for some exceptions) the joy and value of mutuality (one-flesh union) and the procreation and nurture of children.

Given the complex cultural diversity and social history of 2,000 years of Christian history, some might think the above summary is far too simple—that it is simplistic. Some will object that it ignores important negative aspects of traditional Christian sexual attitudes.

For example, some Christian theologians viewed human sexuality, especially sexual pleasure, with great suspicion, associating it with sin. For them, procreation was the only excuse for sex. In fact, theological affirmation of one-flesh mutuality and pleasure possible through sex is relatively recent. Also, traditional sexual attitudes taught men and women to consider males to be superior to women, because supposedly they are more rational. A third troubling aspect of traditional western sexual attitudes and practice is a double standard which allowed males freedom for sexual experience denied to women. A fourth is that the traditional Christian sex ethic functioned within and/or expressed destructive dichotomies and hierarchies which pitted men over women, soul/spirit over body, reason over nature, white over nonwhite. This framework of destructive dichotomies, sometimes referred to as "patriarchy," allegedly underlies other evils like racism, heterosexism and homophobia, colonialism, ageism, and ecological destruction. Therefore, for many people the "traditional Christian sexual ethic" is a very ambiguous heritage indeed.

Certainly, it is overly simple to summarize the 2,000 year history of Christian sexual teaching in three simple points of heterosexuality, marriage, and the goods of procreation and mutuality. What is authentically Christian and what is less than Christian in traditional teaching is open for debate. One must be wary, however, of claiming that all the evils of patriarchy, sexism, homophobia, and so forth are based in the Bible and the Christian religion. Are these problems essential to the Bible and Christian beliefs? Or, are they deformations of biblical teaching, properly interpreted? Double standards and patriarchalism are also features of Japanese, Indian, and Arab cultures. This fact greatly weakens the claim that the alleged faults of "traditional sexual morality" are due only to the Bible and Christian beliefs.

In any case, in this chapter, we do not intend to resolve the question of how the "traditional Christian sexual ethic" should be defined. Rather, we have the more limited task of arguing for the three central norms—that full sexual intimacy between Christians should occur in the context of a lifelong, faithful marriage bond between a man and a woman—since these norms are challenged by the alternative sexual ethic in the church today.

Roots of the Traditional Christian Sex Ethics

The traditional Christian sexual ethic has three roots. The first is the Bible. The second is the natural moral insight of humankind as it reflects on sexuality in relation to the whole of life. The third is the theological reflection on the meaning of sexual relations for Christian disciples in God's church.

Biblical texts. The first two chapters of Genesis depict God's purposes in creating humankind in God's own image—man in relation to woman, for the blessing of procreation and one-flesh union. This is an important biblical source for traditional Christian sexual morality. Specific passages that explicitly prohibit fornication, adultery, and homosexual behavior provide a second important Biblical source. A third source is Jesus' teaching about marriage and divorce, citing the Genesis creation stories. Fourth is Paul's teaching in Romans 1 that homosexual behavior is one symptom of a sinful creation fallen away from God's creative purposes for humanity. Taken together, the specific Biblical passages present clear, consistent, and theologically coherent teaching that heterosexual relating is God's will for humankind, not homosexual acts, fornication, or adultery.

The Biblical Framework. Even more important than the specific texts dealing with sexual behavior is the framework for all the Bible's sexual teaching. Biblical authors typically set moral imperatives in the larger religious context of God's relationship to humankind. Biblical moral rules are not intended as ends in themselves but to guide the common life of God's people in a particular way. The moral teaching seeks to shape the common life so that it reflects nothing less than the character and nature of God, which God makes known to those called into a covenant relationship. Thus, the primary function of biblical moral rules, whether in the Holiness Code (Leviticus 17-26), the Decalogue, the Prophetic writings, the Sermon on the Mount, Paul's letters and the rest of the New Testament, is **witness,** or even more radically, **a moral sharing in the holy nature and character of God.** Of all biblical moral rules, including those prescribing sexual morality, the theme of the Holiness Code holds true: "You shall be holy, for I the Lord your God am holy."[191]

> *The moral teaching seeks to shape the common life so that it reflects nothing less than the character and nature of God . . .*

Natural Moral Law. A second root of the traditional Christian sexual ethic is the Greco-Roman tradition of natural moral law. This perspective evaluated human sexual powers in relation to human nature, the human race and the common good. It was accepted into Christian thinking by early church theologians.

One possible confusion needs to be avoided at the beginning. The perspective of natural moral law is not the same as the perspective of empirical natural and social science. Empirical science asks what sexual phenomena appear in nature and society and what causes these phenomena. The natural moral law perspective asks what basic goods of human life are obtainable through sexual practices, and which sexual practices and rules guide humans toward their full human flourishing.

The confusion is caused by the word "natural" which appears in both "natural science" and "natural moral law." Eliminating the confusion is important because some people think that whatever appears in nature must be what God wills, so that the laws of nature are identical with the natural moral law. We can illustrate the difference by an example. That some people are genetically predisposed to alcohol abuse is, arguably, an empirical fact. Substance abuse, however, is not a practice which promotes and protects human flourishing. In short, what *is* should not always be equated with what *ought* to be.

Human Sexual Potential

One argument in favor of the traditional Christian norms of sexual morality is that they promote the rich human goods potentially present in human sexual powers better than any alternatives. Therefore, these norms promote human actualization and the common good. In other words, common moral insight commends something close to traditional Christian sexual norms, because they guide people into those practices which actualize their personal good and promote the good of the human race. This defence of traditional Christian sexual norms appeals to general human moral reason and experience.

Traditional Christian sexual norms (affirming heterosexual relations, a marital covenant and sexual fidelity) in fact do protect and promote personal actualization and the good of the human race.

First these norms direct people into those sexual relationships in which *both* the goods of procreation and one-flesh communion can be sought *simultaneously and with mutual reinforcement*. Some same-sex genital relationships might help persons experience and share the good of personal communion. Some might argue that the typical gay homosexual activity of anal intercourse connotes subhuman relating more than interpersonal encounter. But one cannot simply dismiss the moving statements of gays and lesbians about the personal fulfillment they experience in their sexual partnerships. Yet, it cannot be denied that even the most mutual and caring same-sex genital activity is in principle closed to human sexuality's potential for procreation. Heterosexual intercourse within a stable covenant, by contrast, does open the partners to *both* the specifically sexual goods of interpersonal communion and procreation, *at the same time*. Granted, some heterosexual couples may be physically unable to conceive children, or given certain circumstances, ought not to become parents. But only faulty reasoning would make these exceptions to the procreative possibility inherent in heterosexual intercourse the basis of a moral principle that procreation is irrelevant to sexual morality.

Heterosexual intercourse, therefore, can set procreation of new life in a context of interpersonal mutuality and equality. Such intercourse directs the pursuit of individual pleasure and interpersonal mutuality to the wider concerns of the whole human community. In short, such intercourse opens the human partners to the fullest potential of human sexuality and engages their whole identity as persons and moral agents.

Granted, such heterosexual relations, more than homosexual acts or in contrast to heterosexual acts which consistently avoid procreation, place great moral demands on human maturity and moral responsibility. But isn't that another way of saying that these traditional norms protect and promote the fullest potential of human actualization?

Evidence From Abandoning Traditional Norms

One can make this same point by examining the pain and suffering caused when people engage in sexual intercourse in defiance of the norms of traditional Christian sexual ethics. Observe the hurt, pain and burden on society caused by sexual relations not governed by the norms of heterosexuality, marriage, and fidelity.

For one thing, sexual relations outside of a faithful marriage covenant often conceive new life without providing a secure, loving context to receive it. The world abortion rate, with all the personal suffering and trauma (especially for women) it represents, testifies to this harm. Also, full sexual intimacy within tentative commitments threatens both parties, but perhaps women especially, with the suffering of separation or rejection, if the other partner decides to break off the relationship. Further, real sex, in contrast to romantic renditions of it, is fraught with possibility of hurt; sexual relations involve us at our most vulnerable levels. Human vulnerability is better protected inside covenants of fidelity and permanence than outside of them.

Further, the epidemic of sexually transmitted diseases caused by the great increase of nonmarital sexual relations demonstrates the individual and social harm such relationships cause. Anal intercourse, a typical form of male homosexual genital sex, is physically dangerous, exposing the partners to the dangers of venereal diseases, including AIDS. Given the unreliability of even "safe sex," advocating physically dangerous forms of genital intercourse and/or multiple sex partners is simply morally irresponsible.

The human body and its physical organs also bear witness for common moral insight to wholesome sexual norms. The sexual organs of males and females relate to one another complementarily. A man or woman whose sexual organs do not correspond to their sexual orientation suffers a real lack in integrity and wholeness. Granted, as we have already acknowledged, same-sex partners can experience authentic mutuality and express real caring. Yet common moral intuition perceives something "wrong" when a person's sexual organs do not correspond to affective sexual desire: Body and psyche are not as fully integrated as in heterosexual orientation.

The Moral Evil of Homophobia

This moral intuition, valid as it is in itself, has led people in the past, including Christians, to ridicule and otherwise persecute homosexual persons. Even Christians have called homosexual persons "queer," to mention only one of the odious epithets. Such persecution, often fueled by homophobia (an irrational fear and hatred of homosexual persons) is evil and morally wrong. It has no place in the church. The gay and lesbian liberation movements inside and outside the churches perform the great service of prophetically challenging traditional Christian persecution and injustice directed toward homosexual persons.

> *Such persecution, often fueled by homophobia (an irrational fear and hatred of homosexual persons) is evil and morally wrong.*

This said, however, natural moral insight correctly senses a lack of wholeness inherent in a person whose sexual affection and physical sexual organs do not correspond to each other. For this reason, persons with a same-sex orientation deserve our empathy and support. These individuals know, in a basic area of life, the suffering of threatened wholeness, and must also endure unjustified ridicule and persecution.

In summary, a second basis and root of the traditional Christian sexual norms of heterosexuality, marriage, and fidelity is common moral reason. Common moral insight discerns that sexual norms should acknowledge, protect, and promote the rich human goods of sexuality, which include both procreation and one-flesh communion. This the traditional Christian moral norms do in an exemplary way.

Some people would object to this appeal to natural moral reason as unnecessary or irrelevant for Christians, because the Bible is all Christians need to learn God's moral imperatives. We would argue that general moral insights into wholesome sexual norms are important to Christian sexual teaching.

The reasons are that God created human nature and called it good; that God reclaims the whole creation, including its physical aspects, from sin and destruction in Jesus' death and resurrection; that God wills eternal communion with his human creatures. Our God is a very material God, one who creates and loves the creation. Christians, therefore, should not scorn humanity's God-given insights into what promotes, provides, and protects human flourishing.

Further, the appeal to natural moral insight conforms to the tradition of Anglican theology and morality. For example, Richard Hooker, in the first Book of his great work *Laws of Ecclesiastical Polity,* presents a rich appeal to the insights of moral reason. Thus, Christian ethics, and especially Anglican ethics, properly looks to common human moral intuition concerning sexuality as one basis for moral teaching.

Sexual Union as an Aspect of Discipleship

A third source and basis for affirming the traditional Christian sexual ethic is the Christian's relation to God, as illumined by basic Christian beliefs. In this section we are not adopting the perspective of common moral insight or the Bible alone but rather viewing sexual relating in the framework of God's love to us in Jesus Christ and our sharing as disciples, through our sexual powers, in God's gift of himself.

From this perspective the church is the proper context for evaluating Christian sexual practices. That is, the church's purpose of worship and witness to God known in Jesus Christ sets the agenda for Christian sexual norms. A Christian's sexual practices are an important aspect of moral participation in God's life in Jesus Christ and of the witness which this participation involves.

The author of Ephesians writes from this perspective. In Chapter 5 he says that the love between husband and wife and their one-flesh union are a mystery which refers beyond itself to Christ and the church. The author is teaching here that God gathers the love and sexual union of husband and wife into the circle of God's relation to the church so that in that circle sexual relations share in and show forth God's self-giving love.

One can expand this basic idea of marriage as a human sign which opens people to a moral participation in God's own life. We can perceive that spiritually heterosexual relations have an especially rich potential for serving the church as a human sign of God's self-giving love in Christ and the Holy Spirit. First, the believer's one-flesh union of sexual intercourse images God's self-giving to the Christian as Holy Spirit, making the human body God's temple. Second, dual sexuality (male and female in relation) and sexual fidelity image for the spouses, for the church, and for the world God's covenant fidelity, focused in Jesus Christ, the Savior. And, extending the imaging power of heterosexual union in relation to God the creator, Christians in their sexual union image God the creator when their sexual unions are pro-creative (in other words, creative on behalf of God.) Heterosexual relations in a lifelong, faithful covenant open to procreation allow disciples to let their sexuality share in and show forth the generative, covenantal, uniting love of God more fully than in same-sex or nonmarital relations.

Spiritually heterosexual relations have an especially rich potential for serving the church as a human sign of God's self-giving love in Christ and the Holy Spirit.

I ask the reader to grasp this central point. The traditional norms support those sexual practices that have greatest potential for letting Christians' sexual powers share in and show forth the creating, covenant-making, uniting nature and work of God, which is a fundamental aspect of discipleship. Note, we are not claiming that the traditional norms have the greatest promise for producing obedience to the norms themselves. Challenging Christians with the rigorous norms of procreation (if God allows), heterosexual relating, sexual fidelity, and limiting full sexual union to marriage does not commend itself because it is easy, or obvious, or an instant "life-enhancement."

On the contrary, I am arguing that these norms should be held up because they lift human sexual relating into a new dimension—the plane where human relations and powers share in and show forth the creative, covenant-making, uniting love of the Triune God. God gathers the sexual relations of Christians into his own life, letting them be a means of sharing in and showing forth that life. This is a distinctively Christian, "discipleship" view of sexual relations.

The Alternative Sexual Ethic

Having offered this summary of the traditional Christian sexual ethic, I now turn to an alternative widely promoted in society and in the mainline Christian churches. It lies behind the recommendations in the sexuality section of the Human Affairs Standing Committee's *Blue Book*. It permeates the views of those advocating full sexual intimacy for persons never married, for divorced people, and for same-sex partners.

We must admit from the start that it is overly simple to speak of **the** alternative sexual morality today. There are several: the so-called Playboy Philosophy, the ethic of sexual self-actualization, and what has been called "the personalist sex ethic."[192] The first accepts the modern notion of sex as a drive or pressure seeking release and promising pleasure. This Playboy Philosophy attacks the "medieval" idea that sex is only or primarily for procreation and the "Victorian" idea that sex should be unmentioned, repressed, and sublimated. On the contrary, says this ethic, "use sex for pleasure; the only two moral prohibitions are coercing your partner or conceiving an unwanted child."

The second is the ethic of self-actualization. According to this view individual life enhancement is the test for sexual choices. This and the Playboy Philosophy are so individualistic that neither has gained much headway in the Christian Church.

Much more influential is what Philip Turner calls the personalist sex ethic. This sexual ethic is the chief contender for the minds and hearts of Episcopalians and other Christians in the main-line churches today.[193]

The Personalist Sex Ethic

What are its chief tenets? The first is that the most important thing about human sexuality is not sexual organs or particular sexual acts but personhood and interpersonal relationships. The cardinal tenet of the personalist sex ethic, in fact, is that the religious and human meaning of sexual relationships is mutuality and justice, the experience of mutual caring, giving and receiving of pleasure, the joy of mutuality, and the promotion of human equality in sexual relations and in all relationships. Sexuality is not about procreation primarily, nor about "natural" or "unnatural" acts; sexuality is about relationships. Sexuality is a primary way, perhaps **the** primary way, humans reach out from their individual existence to touch others and to promote justice (in the sense of equality). Thus the underlying premise is that sexual relations should be guided by the aim of human fulfillment now, **understood as the giving and receiving of caring, and as experiencing and promoting just relationships.**

Sexual Immorality According to the Alternative Ethic

If sexuality is to enhance life now by promoting respect and caring, what does this sexual ethic consider immoral? First and foremost, any sexual relationship which lacks equality and mutuality is immoral. Such relationships intrinsically block the coming to personal wholeness of either of the partners. Thus, any relationship involving coercion, harassment, or exploitation is wrong. Included in these, of course, would be relations between adults and children, an intrinsically unequal relationship. Relations influenced by patriarchal attitudes regarding the superiority of men over women would be wrong, as would any merely casual or promiscuous sexual relationship. Such relationships cannot really be the context for caring and mutuality.

Further, any sexual relationship in which pleasure is the *only* goal of either or even both partners is probably immoral. To engage habitually in sexual intercourse for pleasure alone loses sight of the caring and interpersonal communion that sexual relations should express, according to this sexual ethic. Also, it contradicts justice, since to treat one partner as simply a means for one's own pleasure does not affirm the equal worth of the partner.

What does this sexual ethic imply about who may enter full sexual relationships? One thing is clear: Full sexual intimacy need not be confined to heterosexual partners. Same-sex partners can express respect and caring in their sexual relationships; arguably, same-sex relations promote equality more easily that heterosexual relations burdened by unequal role expectations and sexism. Further, a vow of lifelong sexual fidelity is not necessary for partners to experience caring and express respect. Some sort of commitment is probably required for a relationship to express caring and respect; but certainly not a lifelong, sexually exclusive relationship, argue defenders of this ethic.

Some proponents of the new ethic claim that married partners can have respectful and caring relations with partners who are not their spouses. They call for a non-sexually exclusive redefinition of marital fidelity. Persons who are married, so long as they are sufficiently honest and open with their spouses, can morally enter full sexual relations with others and experience all the richness of human sexuality: equality, mutuality, expression of caring, and pleasure.

The Personalist Sex Ethic and the Sexual Revolution

To understand this personalist sex ethic more fully, one needs to see it within the cultural context of the sexual revolution of the nineteenth and twentieth centuries. While the personalist sex ethic is not merely a product or reflection of modern assumptions, an appreciation for the broader social and cultural changes helps us understand it.

> *To understand this personalist sex ethic more fully, one needs to see it within the cultural context of the sexual revolution . . .*

One premise for the personalist sex ethic, obviously, is the modern mindset which locates sexuality in the private sphere where the drama of personal fulfillment (understood as self-acceptance and deep, meaningful relationships with another human being) is played out. The goal of sexual relations, according to this personalist sex ethic, is personal life-enhancement—including self-acceptance, ability to enter into relationships marked by commitment, caring, pleasure, joy, loyalty, and the integration of willing, thinking, feeling, and bodily vitality. Sexuality fulfills its purpose as part of the empowering of human personhood. A second premise, which is in keeping with the emancipative movements of the age, is the value of promoting just (in the sense of equal) relationships in all aspects of society, including the sexual sphere. Thus, the two major norms of the personalist sex ethic—caring and justice (equality)—correspond to basic features of modernity.

What larger cultural context, then, illuminates the personal sex ethic? What first comes to people's minds when they think of the sexual revolution are the remarkable *changes in sexual behavior* in modern times.[194] One obvious change is the new openness in discussing sexual matters. Sex is now a topic for genteel conversation.

Greater frequency of sexual intercourse outside of marriage and at an ever younger age is another manifestation of the sexual revolution. A recent *Washington Post* article reports 27 percent of females and 33 percent of males "become sexually active" by age 15.[195] By age 19 the percentages jump to 75 and 86, respectively. Parish clergy report that nine of ten couples coming for marriage preparation are already living together.

The use of contraceptives, which attempt to separate the unitive from the procreative potentials of sexual intercourse, has increased enormously. This is another decisive feature of the sexual revolution.

Finally, among the new practices which mark the sexual revolution are the shift in sources by which adolescents gain their information about and images of human sexual practices. Now the decisive educators in the society are the mass-mediated pop culture with ads linking sex to products targeting teens, pop music and music videos, and sex education in the public schools. Sexual information and sexual images are intentionally directed by the adult world toward the young, either in a well-intentioned effort to instruct, to entertain, or to sell a product. Adolescents have probably always received much of their sexual knowledge from their peers. Society, however, traditionally assigns to adult family members the role of sexual educators. Today, other adults claim that duty and right.

Attitudes of the Sexual Revolution

Beneath such changed practices, promoting them and making them intelligible, are *changed attitudes*. Any account of the sexual revolution must mention these.

One basic shift is the centrality accorded sexuality in the modern mind. Sigmund Freud's sexual theories symbolize this important facet of the sexual revolution. Working with a pressure-cooker model of the human psyche, Freud thought of human sexuality as a central dimension of what he called the Id, an impersonal and basic vitality expressing itself as human libido seeking pleasure. Freud, as much as any modern thinker, persuaded modern people to think of sexuality not as an appetite (a desire that contributed to human and social flourishing), but as an undirected drive. Sex is, for Freud, an impersonal, fundamental drive whose management through the Oedipal or Electra stages greatly influences psychic health. The sexual drive can be repressed, sublimated, or expressed, but it cannot be denied. To deny this drive is to risk having its vitality overwhelm the self. On the other hand, some popular attitudes hold that its vitality is so basic that getting in touch with one's own sexuality or with the sexuality of another promises profound life-enhancement and even the experience of a psychic redemption. In either case, sex is at the center of identity; it may be that center.

The expression of libidinous energy brings pleasure, whether the sexual drive is expressed in relation to a member of the opposite sex, the same sex, an animal, or an object. Freud pioneered the now widely accepted notion that negotiating our sexual drives is one of the most important tasks of early human development, if not the most important task.

Private Sex

A second change marking the sexual revolution was the privatizing of human sexuality. As the industrial revolution advanced, it encouraged the mental habit of dividing the life-world into a private and public sphere. In the public sphere belonged the business corporation and other bureaucratic institutions of government, education, military, and increasingly, health care. To the private sphere belonged the zone of personal choice and preference: the realms of marriage, sexual preference, recreation, and other aspects of personal "life-style."[196]

If the public sphere is impersonal, governed by utilitarian reason, the norms of efficiency, contractual relations, and competition, the private sphere is the realm of interpersonal intimacy, belonging, personal affirmation, and acceptance. Sexuality, thus, has increasingly been thought of as a realm of individual and personal life-enhancement, usually involving a "significant other" but not essentially related to the public world or the common good. The procreative potential of sexual intercourse, linking human sexuality to family, community and society, was increasingly viewed as separable from (by means of birth control) and secondary to its potential to promote interpersonal communion. This point is absolutely fundamental for the ethical debate today in the Christian churches.

Emancipated Sexuality

To understand the changed attitudes toward sexuality in the sexual revolution, we must also remember that emancipation from authoritarian Christian control marks most areas of modern human life, sexuality included. The story of modern western culture can be titled "Emancipation." One sector of intellectual life after another —first natural science, then philosophy, political theory, economics, and the arts—broke free from the church's intellectual control. Social change has been the story of revolutionary emancipation.

Human sexuality has been caught up in this dynamic of liberation. This emancipation has focused on women's being freed from the political constraints and cultural biases of patriarchalism and sexism. Women have attained political power and affirmed the value and uniqueness of their own sexuality.

One of the most powerful appeals of the personalist ethic, which is proposed as a replacement for traditional sexual morality in the church, is that it would further the emancipation of both male and female sexuality from past oppressive hierarchies.

The New Paradigm

Finally, we don't begin to grasp the full depth of new attitudes toward human sexuality until we perceive that much current thinking about sexuality occurs within a paradigm shift in our understanding of reality as a whole. If the traditional paradigm told us to make clear distinctions between human beings and the world of nature, between masculine and feminine, between subject and object, between God and the world, the new paradigm asks us to think of reality as developing and interrelated. The new paradigm, citing for support subatomic physics and relativity theory, tells us to stop envisioning reality as divided into distinct categories in hierarchical relationship. Rather, we should envision everything as related to everything else; beings are not opposed to each other but in polar relationship.

Further, we are to think of reality as a life-flow, as a process rather than an order, a process increasing in diversity, complexity, and richness of interconnectedness. In the perspective of the new paradigm, the old clear distinctions between male and female, heterosexual and homosexual, masculine and feminine are *passe*; to cling to them betrays defensiveness and a desire to control. Those championing the paradigm shift urge us all to drop these distinctions and affirm new emerging patterns of selfhood and relationship.

Plausibility of the Personalist Ethic

Before we discuss the defects of the personalist sex ethic, let us first ask why this sexual morality, which views sexual intercourse as a means of cementing just and caring relationships, is so enthusiastically accepted by many intelligent, concerned people inside and outside the church. First, in a culture filled with much loneliness and anonymity, a culture that has reduced people to mere functions, interpersonal intimacy is experienced as a great good. People invest the private sphere with great hope: It is the stage for the drama of the personhood seeking empowerment and self-expression, the source of relationships in which people find acceptance and affirmation, the place where people touch each other intimately.

> *[L]et us first ask why this sexual morality . . . is so enthusiastically accepted by many intelligent, concerned people inside and outside the church.*

Second, the personalist sex ethic highlights real failures in the church, which has upheld the traditional sex ethic. The divorce rate among Christians, including clergy, is rising. Is the traditional sex ethic working today? Don't Christian divorces indicate that it isn't?

Also, the inequality, oppression, and exploitation of women—all proper targets of feminist protest—appear imbedded in traditional Christian teaching on sex. Paul wrote that women were inferior to men, should have no authority over men, and should keep silent in church. Some religious authorities opposed women's suffrage; Christian theologians have charged women with greater responsibility than men for original sin.

Additionally, homophobia pervades the church, breeding its most virulent expressions—physical attack and even killing of persons known or thought to be homosexually oriented. Christians supporting the traditional sex ethic have often succumbed to homophobia.

Finally, the personalist sex ethic appears to champion the biblical language of love and justice. Love is a central theme of the personalist sex ethic. Love, in this ethic, means unconditional affirmation as well as self-acceptance. And do not sexual relations that express deep caring and tenderness serve as exemplary vehicles for such love? Justice is also a central biblical theme. Old Testament prophets spoke God's Word calling for justice to flow like a flood through the life of God's people. The vocabulary of the personalist sex ethic seems to resonate not just with today's prizing of personhood and intimacy but with the Bible's imperatives of love and justice.

Assessment of the Personalist Sex Ethic

The sexual revolution and the personalist ethic involve fundamental shifts in morality, understanding, and behavior. As just indicated, we would claim that many of these changes should be affirmed by a Christian sex ethic today. For instance, we should welcome and integrate into Christian teaching the new knowledge about human sexuality gained through the physical and social sciences. We should also affirm the wholesomeness of the more open attitudes toward human sexuality. Much suffering was caused by treating human sexuality as a taboo. We certainly should affirm the pleasure and the mutuality possible through sexual relations. Sexuality is not just a necessary evil for the sake of procreation as some pessimistic theologians have taught. A contemporary Christian sex ethic should also affirm the concern for equality and mutuality ideals of the alternative sex ethic.

We would claim, however, that a creative reappropriation of the traditional Christian sexual norms of heterosexuality, covenant faithfulness, and openness to the goods of procreation and mutuality can affirm all these good aspects of the sexual revolution and the alternative sexual ethic.

Yet the personalist sex ethic is not without its problems. Indeed, the remainder of this chapter points out not only some contradictions in this alleged Christian sex ethic but also its fundamental contradiction to some basic Christian concerns.

Ignoring Procreation. One basic problem of the alternative sex ethic is that it relegates the procreative potential of human sexuality to a place of theological and moral indifference. The personalist sex ethic reduces the value of sexual relations to being a vehicle for caring and equality. In so doing it ignores the fact that human sexuality, in its physical dimension, inherently concerns procreation. This fact about human sexuality means that the personalist sex ethic's claim of concern for the whole person cannot be taken at face value.

> *One suspects that the personalist ethic may simply share our middle-class perspective that procreation is expensive and technologically dispensable.*

Human wholeness, whatever else it means, requires that in any discussion of our lives we take our embodiment as seriously as our mental intentions. We are embodied selves, not free-floating minds. Physically, our sexuality involves sexual organs that are incomplete and lose their intelligibility when considered in terms of the individual alone. Male sex organs gain their intelligibility in relation to female sex organs and vice versa. And these organs gain their physical intelligibility in relation to the procreative potential of human sexuality.

The personalist sex ethic ignores or discounts this aspect of human sexuality. In fact, the personalist sex ethic is amazingly disembodied and spiritualistic. For it, the sexed body is merely an instrument for expressing moral principles or attitudes of equality and caring; the specifically sexual potential of procreation is irrelevant. One suspects that the personalist ethic may simply share our middle-class perspective that procreation is expensive and technologically dispensable. Thus the personalist ethic may reflect more than it cares to acknowledge of the proprietary values of middle-class elites.

Viewing the procreative potential of human sexuality as inessential to its ethic contradicts the full reality of human sexuality. It also breeds gross injustice in sexual relationships. Heterosexual intercourse, barring infertility or other problems, is inherently procreative. If a couple able to conceive children doesn't take positive steps to avoid it, procreation of new life is always a possibility during the woman's fertile period.

This intrinsic procreative potential of heterosexual intercourse, combined with the many reasons contraceptive means don't work, accounts for the many thousands of unwanted pregnancies which occur annually in the U.S. alone. Such pregnancies wreak great injustice on the new lives conceived under these conditions. Either these new lives will be destroyed through "therapeutic" abortion, or if they are brought to term, they will be born to parents with less than ideal relationships. The personalist ethic ignores sexuality's procreative potential by promoting the falsehood that only "caring" and "equality" are morally important in sexual relations. Thus, this ethic unfortunately promotes gross injustice toward new human life and mothers. The personalist sex ethic adds fuel to this injustice when it justifies sexual intercourse between partners not married to each other.

Further, by ignoring the procreative potential of sexuality, the personalist ethic effectively fails to call people to a most demanding and important horizon of love possible through sexual relations. Christian love involves the determination to be for another. Giving life to another and nurturing that life is a profound act of self-giving. By concentrating so much on the good of mutuality, the personalist ethic actually promotes a rather self-enclosed, self-regarding understanding of love. Same-sex relations, also approved by the personalist ethic, even intensify the image of sexual relations as narcissistic, like loving like.

"Commitment." A second basic problem with the personalist ethic is the instability inherent in its notion of commitment. The personalist ethic insists that full sexual intimacy should occur only in "committed relationships." Yet, it usually leaves the meaning of "commitment" vague, something for the partners to decide. This vagueness opens people, especially women, to deep hurt.

The reason is that sexual relationships offer both the promise of great personal fulfillment and the occasion for great hurt. Sexual relations are among the most vulnerable aspects of our lives, opening us to real intentional and unintentional trauma. The traditional sexual ethic, by insisting on a lifelong, sexually exclusive relationship, helps partners in this respect. Partners have a secure, stable space to work through sexual problems unburdened by the fear that dissatisfaction is sufficient reason to end the relationship.

This is not so in the personalist sexual ethic. It affirms commitment *as a means* to joyful and just sex. But as we said, sexual relationships involving people in all their complexity seldom provide uninterrupted bliss to either, much less to both partners. Practically speaking, using commitment as a *means* to attain the joy of sex undermines the stability of such relationships. After all, if one or both partners are hurt or dissatisfied, one or both are justified, even morally obliged, to end the commitment. Thus, contrary to first impressions, the personalist sex ethic's stress on commitment actually promotes unstable and undependable relationships. If the life-long vow of traditional marriage proves so fragile today, how much more breakable are these "committed relationships" championed by the personalist ethic?

A Troubling Logic. Third, the personalist sex ethic must be faulted for promoting a destructive confusion between sexual intimacy and caring relationships. By making intimacy and mutuality a key, if not the only, justification for sexual intimacy, this ethic promotes the identification of sex with caring. One crude example of this confusion is the young man who coerces his girlfriend by saying, "If you really love me, you will sleep with me." Another is the incestuous father who says, "I wanted my daughter to learn sex from someone who really loves her." Still another is the common advice those promoting the personalist sex ethic give to teenagers: "If you really love and care for your friend, it is all right to sleep with him or her, so long as you practice safe sex."

The personalist sex ethic does not intend to promote incestuous sex and it decries unjust (coercive, hierarchical) sexual relations. Its defenders might respond to our critique by insisting that every sexual relation should be between equals (which may be an impossible goal using any strict definition of equality) thus excluding any relationship between partners of unequal power. Yet, careful reflection shows this thinking actually would promote the sexualization of all caring relations by insisting that the meaning of sex is intimacy, communion, and mutuality.

Relations between friends, parents and adult children, teachers and students, therapists and clients, pastors and parishioners can be deeply caring. These relationships can be marked by mutual respect and can occur between consenting adults. Yet sound moral wisdom teaches that these relationships, so basic to social life, ought not be genital-sexual relationships. But the personalist ethic condones their becoming such. The logic of insisting that sexuality is for expressing communion and caring easily becomes the logic which argues that caring and respect justify (and even require?) sexual intimacy.

In our sex-obsessed culture we need parental, sibling, friendship, teaching, pastoral, and therapeutic sex-free zones. We need areas of our lives that are not charged with sexual expectations and implications. The personalist sex ethic does little to protect these relationships from inappropriate sexualization and actually undermines their integrity in this regard.

Human-Centered, Not God-Centered Gospel. Finally, the personalist sex ethic has a deficient view of the Gospel itself. The premise of this ethic is that God's love is God's affirmation of us. This means God wants to empower our personhood and wants us to empower others' personhood. We obey God when we affirm ourselves and others to be "all that they can be."

Obviously this view of God's love is grossly inadequate, when judged by the Bible and Christian tradition. First, God's love is not an affirmation of the self we want to be. God's love is defined by the sacrificial love of the Christ who suffered and died to redeem us from sin and open a new relationship to God.

God's love is not an affirmation of the self we want to be. God's love is defined by the sacrificial love of the Christ who suffered and died to redeem us from sin and open a new relationship to God.

Second, God's love is ultimately God's gift of himself, accomplished as God gathers our sexual powers and all other wholesome aspects of our lives, to be means of sharing in and showing forth his creativity, covenant faithfulness, and unity. God's saving purpose is not simply to perfect our human vitality in history as an end in itself; it is to transfigure our lives in Christ with the glory of his own life.

The premise of the personalist sex ethic is a human-centered reduction of the Gospel to God affirming us. Thereby the personalist sexual ethic shows itself to be more a reflection of modern human-centered philosophies than an implication of the Bible. The Bible witnesses to the centrality and sovereignty of God and to God's love as God's sharing his life with us.

Conclusion

The Christian church has something to learn from the proposed personalist sex ethic; Christians should not simply dismiss it. But Christians must "test the spirits," drawing from the personalist sex ethic its valid insights but not letting its faulty premises and teachings undermine the truth of traditional Christian sexual teaching. Such discriminating thinking would be a creative reception of traditional Christian sexual teaching for our church today. As it stands, unfortunately, the sexuality section in the Human Affairs *Blue Book* does not provide the Episcopal Church with such a creative reception of valid Christian sexual teaching.

CHAPTER

Non-Traditional Life Styles

Anyone who has been active in pastoral ministry over the past two decades is fully aware of the degree to which parishioners' life-styles depart from the model of lifelong heterosexual monogamy. My own experience during eight years of parochial ministry included the following situations and many others: the young man who asked me to tell his family members about his gay life-style because he was afraid of how they might respond; the young bride's parents who asked me to advise their daughter to live with rather than marry the fiancé of whom they did not approve; the divorced woman and her lesbian partner who struggled to raise a teenaged son; the middle-aged man who felt that his wife's inability to "keep herself up" as she had when younger was sufficient justification for the taking of a mistress; the young mother who left her husband and children for another man; the young mother who left her husband and children for another woman; the husband who left his family for a gay life style; the lesbian who feared that her partner

Sexual Morality and Pastoral Care

Robert W. Prichard

would leave her for a man; and the father with a more than normal interest in embracing his teenage stepdaughter. Such a list is, I suspect, closer to the rule than to the exception of pastoral life. While there are many stable, traditional, lifelong, heterosexual marriages in the parishes in which I have served, I would say that a significant percentage—perhaps forty percent—of the day-to-day family problems I encountered involved non-traditional life styles.

There is little question that this reality has fueled the search for a new ethic in the past two decades. Parish clergy recognize many wonderful qualities in people with non-traditional life-styles. When pastors recognize need, they are anxious to deal faithfully with such parishioners. What, they ask, can one say to those in such situations?

The Church of England's *Book of Common Prayer* had one solution to the problem—an office known as the Commination. Read on Ash Wednesday and other occasions as directed by the bishop, the service included a recitation of Old Testament condemnations from Deuteronomy 28. The priest recited nine such curses, and the congregation responded "Amen" to each. Included in the list of those condemned were "he that lieth with his neighbor's wife," "adulterers," and "fornicators."[197]

Surely this approach would not work today. A major portion of the people who compose an ordinary Episcopal congregation would never confide in any priest who took such a route, if indeed they would remain in contact with the church he or she served.

An Interim Suspension of Judgment

In the first or second year after my ordination, I recall counseling an angelic looking couple in their mid-twenties who planned to marry. Their youthful, healthy appearance radiated wholesomeness.

I knew they, like the majority of couples of their age or older whom I have prepared for marriage, were living together. In one of our counseling sessions I invited them to talk about the way in which they met. What followed was a lurid tale that might have come from Henry Fielding's *Tom Jones* or Daniel Defoe's *Amorous Adventures of Moll Flanders*. Theirs was a story of casual sex, of sleeping with one another's best friends in order to "get even," of drug use, and of scrapes with the police. I tried to listen with seriousness and interest, for the story did bring important insights to the relationship of the couple. The couple noted my amazement and indeed embarrassment about some of what they had to say.

I think of that embarrassment now, because I notice that I no longer have it. A few years of parish ministry are sufficient to banish it forever. The encounter with a real congregation brings the priest face to face with so many moral and sexual permutations that it is soon impossible to be surprised. The priest has already heard it all.

Clergy respond to that loss of naivete in a variety of ways. Some grow disillusioned and leave the ministry altogether. Others gladly receive the knowledge of that behavior as sufficient justification to begin (or persist in) acting the same way. More common, however, is an interim suspension of judgment, a basic decision to accept all that comes without comment and without censure. The priest, in effect, agrees to enter into the world of the parishioner in order to minister to that parishioner.

Confusing the Interim with the Ultimate

The strategy of withholding judgment is so much a part of Episcopal pastoral styles that it is almost a given in the denomination. Parishioners and the population at large assume, and with good reason, that they can enter into dialogue with Episcopal clergy about almost anything. A member of Dignity, the Catholic gay and lesbian support group, commented as much to me in a recent phone conversation. He said that he did not expect or find much support from Roman Catholic clergy, but knew that he always had the Episcopal Church as a resource. Episcopal clergy were willing to listen.

While the adopting of this style is an effective strategy for gaining the confidence and trust of parishioners, it does leave some unanswered questions. What, for example, is the exact status of this suspension of judgment? What happens when the interim is over, and trust and confidence have been gained? When it is the priest's turn to speak, what will she or he say?

At this point clergy are most divided. Some, imitating the therapeutic style popularized by psychologist Carl Rogers, try to avoid the problem by saying, in effect, that the interim should have no end. The priest listens and waits for the counseled individual to make final decisions, for no one is interested in the priest's advice and opinion.

But that is not precisely true. People do disregard clergical advice and clergical examples with great regularity, but they also follow them in surprising ways. People with non-standard sexual lives do, after all, seek out the conversation of the clergy of the church. Whether consciously or not, they are seeking something. They also take cues from clergy behavior. (If you doubt this, notice the inevitable rise in parishioner divorces following the breakup of a clergy marriage.)

Others, recognizing the difficulty of perpetual silence, try to absolutize the reservation of judgment, making it not only a pastoral strategy, but also the final moral word. The church should bless all things, they seem to say. This is the route taken in John S. Spong's *Living in Sin* and, to a lesser degree, the 1991 *Blue Book* report of the Standing Commission on Human Affairs. The church should bless mutually caring homosexual and heterosexual sexual arrangements, whether or not they hold the promise of permanence.[198] Alternatively, the church should bless gay and lesbian relationships that approximate heterosexual marital fidelity.[199]

There are problems with this approach. The disagreement between Spong's *Living in Sin* and the Standing Commission on Human Affairs's report illustrates the difficulty, for example, in agreeing on precisely which judgments are to be suspended. There is a more serious problem, however—the danger that the church which absolutizes the interim judgment is left with literally nothing to say. Once the acceptance of all things becomes the final word or the absolute value, the priest has no meaningful contribution to make to the lives of those with whom he or she has established a friendship. If fornication and adultery, divorce and marriage, homosexuality and heterosexuality are all equally attractive, what possible word of advice and counsel can the priest provide to the person torn between two such options? Something more is needed.

An Alternative

A number of years ago, I spoke with a couple about marriage. The bride had been married once before. The groom had not. They had been living together for several years, and had, in fact, purchased a home together. I talked with them over the space of a month and found them to be deeply committed to one another. At that time the diocesan bishop required a long supporting letter from the priest and a copy of the final divorce decree with any request for remarriage. I drafted the letter, emphasizing the length and depth of the commitment of the man and the woman.

The bishop's reply came with the return mail. He had circled both the date of the final divorce decree and the date on which I had noted the couple's purchase of a home. Clearly the bride had bought the home with the intended second husband while still married to the first. The bishop made but one comment, "Did you tell them that adultery was wrong?"

The bishop's point was a simple one. It was wonderful that I had gotten to know the couple and had learned of their commitment to one another. It was admirable that I could tell others about their pride in home ownership. I had, in some sense, won a level

> *Those who acknowledge the full power of sin recognize that change in the behavior of parishioners comes only slowly and haltingly.*

of friendship and confidence in them. I needed to use it. It is only the friend, after all, who can really say a hard thing in a way in which it can be heard. The couple needed to know that they would have to rule certain behaviors out of bounds if their relationship were to stand any possibility of lasting. Adultery is destructive and wrong, and they needed desperately to hear that from someone who had won their confidence.

In a curious turn of logic some have come to believe that any behavior that is deep seated and pervasive must not be wrong. If many act in a certain way, those with that point of view argue, it must be a proper behavior. It is a gift given from God, who is after all the creator of all that is. Sin as a result is trivialized; it becomes a behavior that is easily avoided. Sexual addiction, drug use, or alcoholism are not sinful; littering is. Such a conception bears little relationship to the Christian understanding of the pervasive and deepseated sinfulness of human beings, who are bound in sin to such a degree that only the Son of God incarnate is able to redeem them.

Those who acknowledge the full power of sin recognize that change in the behavior of parishioners comes only slowly and haltingly. The raising of a Christian standard of behavior should not be the occasion, therefore, for the expulsion of those who do not meet that standard, but for the beginning of an extended pastoral conversation that will in many cases be lifelong. The young man who tearfully confessed his gay behavior and promised that he would never again visit the gay book and video store where he had casual sex (and had contracted AIDS) may be unable to keep his promise. The lesbian couple who affirm the goodness of close same-sex friendship and the appropriateness of celibacy in such relationships may still return to sexual intimacy. The adulterer may remain faithful for a time, only to return to extramarital affairs. The couple with marital difficulties who had reached a new understanding may resume their arguing.

Even, however, the raising of a standard of behavior and the failure to meet it proclaims the Gospel. Christian life is a story of attempt and failure, of forgiveness and thanksgiving, and of attempt and failure once again. Changes in behavior are always partial and short of perfection. Yet the very effort to live the Christian life and the acceptance of forgiveness when failing to do so is the means by which humans draw closer to the God who is revealed in Jesus Christ.

> *The very effort to live the Christian life and the acceptance of forgiveness when failing to do so is the means by which humans draw closer to the God who is revealed in Jesus.*

Not surprisingly, perhaps, this level of conversation has been for me the point of the most engaging and the deepest pastoral contacts. When talking about the struggle between the desire of one thing and the hope of another, of the conflict of behavior and intention, priest and parishioner come closest to the heart of the Gospel. To stop the mouth of the priest before this point, to make the suspension of judgment absolute, is to rob the content of the Gospel and in the process to impoverish the priest's own spiritual life.

The interim suspension of judgment can never be more than an interim action. It cannot be the last word. When the confidence is won and the friendship made, the pastor who loves the people will begin to suggest the standard of the Gospel.

A Confused Gospel

Some of the advocates of the ordination and blessing of gay and lesbian persons agree that the church cannot stop with the suspension of judgment. Carter Heyward argued precisely this point in her *Touching Our Strength*. "We need sexual ethics," she wrote. "We need an ethical, moral, apprehension of ourselves in relation that can inform our sexual behavior by helping us understand what is right or wrong for us."[200] For her it is not enough simply to argue that all things are equally right.

The position that Carter Heyward and others, including Robert Williams (1955-1992), have taken is a very different position from that of John S. Spong or the Standing Commission on Human Affairs. For Spong and the Standing Commission the interim suspension of judgment has become the final word, leaving the parish priest with little advice or assistance to offer the troubled parishioner. Not so with Heyward and Williams; they have plenty of advice to offer. The advice they offer, however, is quite different from the traditional message of the church.

Heyward, for example, has provided a stinging critique of monogamous marriage. The institution, she argues, entails some benefits, such as financial security and the emotional clarity of a single relationship. Yet it is an institution founded on the premise that one person (the male) owns another (the female), one that often serves as a "canopy for unspoken hurt, lies, and in time, the dissolution of a relationship." Her final judgment, therefore, is that:

> Because monogamy in western culture has such a morally ambiguous history, *it would seem to have little to commend it* to women (or men) of any color who do not wish to be the possession of anyone and who, moreover, are able to participate (economically, culturally, otherwise) in setting the terms of how they shall relate sexually and with whom.[201]

Heyward suggests an alternative to this corrupt institution, which she calls sexual friendship. The sexual friendship need not be exclusive, for there are "ways of being honest and open in relation to two or more lovers over a single period of time." Lesbians have had less success than gay men with such ways of relating, but this, she explains, "may stem from some of the least secure moments, memories, and facts of our lives as sexual objects in heterosexist, racist patriarchy."[202]

For Heyward the exploring of sexual friendship becomes the vehicle through which one encounters the love of God. That exploring becomes

> a process of godding, of moving physically, emotionally, and spiritually together into a strengthening of our capacities to respect and delight in ourselves and others. Crossing boundaries erotically in this way can be a fully incarnate experience of transcendence, in which God comes with us, touching and touched in her deepest places.[203]

Heyward notes the possibility of celibacy, but devotes little time to the topic and avoids the broad value statements that she makes of sexual friendships or monogamy.

Robert Williams, who is quoted in Heyward's book, was, however, more clear about his attitudes. He found both celibacy and monogamy "unnatural," for, he argued, "people are not monogamous. It is crazy to hold this ideal and pretend it's what we're doing and we're not."[204]

Curiously, therefore, Williams and Heyward concur in the rejection of the absolutizing of the suspension of judgment by Bishop Spong and by the Standing Commission on Human Affairs. The church, they agree, cannot simply bracket all areas of human sexuality and avoid the expressing of opinions or the giving of advice. They differ only in the quality of advice that they would give.

If the church is to face the question of sexual morality with seriousness, it will in the end have to choose between one of two courses of action—the traditional sexual ethics of marital fidelity and celibacy, or the new ethic of sexual friendship. Silence seems irresponsible.

The thrust of this volume, of course, is that only one of those two options represents the voice of the church as Christians have heard it over the space of twenty centuries, many of which have been fully as tumultuous as our own. Celibacy and heterosexual marital fidelity are the states of life to which God calls us.

CHAPTER
10

A Contemporary Preoccupation

In the past 10 to 15 years, issues concerning sex and sexuality have assumed more dominant positions in national, diocesan, and local church politics. The national level has the Standing Commission on Human Affairs, and nearly every diocese now has a task force on human sexuality.

By Word and Example: The Church and Moral Education

Elizabeth Zarelli Turner

Questions concerning homosexuality are the most consistent and controversial issues discussed by members of the Standing Commission and the various task forces: Should practicing homosexuals be ordained? Should same sex unions be blessed by the church? Is homosexuality a valid alternative to heterosexuality?

The eruption of the AIDS crisis has also forced churches to confront issues of sex and sexuality, and the responses have been as varied as the denominations themselves. Some churches have essentially dismissed the tragedy of AIDS as an indication of the wrath of God. Some pastors have handed out condoms for "safe sex" from their pulpits on Sunday mornings, while others have burned condoms in response. St. Patrick's Roman Catholic Cathedral in New York City is picketed on an almost weekly basis by members of the gay and lesbian activist organization ACTUP, because Cardinal O'Connor refuses to encourage means of "safe sex." The Episcopal Church (among others) has, correctly I think, approached the AIDS crisis from a primarily pastoral perspective and has supported a variety of AIDS ministries in the dioceses.

Homosexuality and AIDS are not the only issues of concern to the churches. In January 1992, the Centers for Disease Control reported that 54% of high school age respondents had had sexual intercourse. The Centers polled 11,631 students in grades 9-12 from all 50 states, the District of Columbia, Puerto Rico, and the Virgin Islands and found 61% of the boys and 48% of the girls were sexually active. Not surprisingly, the percentages increased with age: 40% of ninth graders, 48% of tenth graders, 57% of eleventh graders, and 72% of twelfth graders.[205] It would be naive and foolish to assume that Episcopal youth are not included among these statistics. For all the controversy surrounding issues of sex and sexuality there is certainly agreement that these statistics are alarming.

The question that confronts us is: What is the church's role in the sexual or moral education of our children? Should the church join forces with schools and parents in the task of sex education? Should we be publishing Christian sex education materials at the national, diocesan, and local levels? Dare we be like ostriches with our heads in the sands of the times, entrusting the sex education of our children to their peers, teachers, and communities?

My contention is that the church should not assume the role of sex educator. Instead, we should provide a moral education by being the Christian community we are called by God to be. We must teach both adults and children the theological significance of relationships between men and women.

St. James' Church

For three years I was the Associate to the Rector for Christian Education at St. James' Church in New York City, responsible for adult and children's programs. The search for appropriate curricula was by far the greatest challenge of that ministry. Lectionary-based curricula did not provide adequate coverage of the Hebrew Scripture, and until the current effort by the Center for the Ministry of Teaching in Virginia, few Episcopal materials offered alternative approaches. Other materials were often not age appropriate for children in upper grades, though biblically sound.

Our solution was to use a combination of materials. The primary and kindergarten classes used another denominational curriculum. Grades 1-5 used a "home grown" version. Our primary goal in these grades was the redressing of the biblical illiteracy for which Episcopalians have a not undeserved reputation. The sixth and seventh graders used the lectionary based curriculum on the assumption that having reached that level they were familiar with the basic stories, and discussing the lesson in class would better equip them to listen to the sermon and lessons at the morning's worship service.

I had no more than 26 or 27 weeks of classes in which to cover more material than was humanly possible.

Our emphasis every fall was on stories from the Hebrew Scriptures. From Advent through the remainder of the academic year we followed the life and ministry of Jesus. Because Pentecost so often falls near the conclusion of the program year, however, there was a significant shortchanging of the ministry and teaching of St. Paul, the apostles, and the early church.

We also used "home grown" eighth-grade confirmation materials. That class was the year for attempting the impossible: a summary of biblical materials, instruction on the Episcopal Church, the sacraments, the *Book of Common Prayer*, and several sessions on "ethics." Needless to say, a few weeks on ethics didn't ripple the water of a moral education.

Each spring and summer as I sat down with a calendar of the following church school year and a list of what I would like to see covered, I faced a dilemma. I had no more than 26 or 27 weeks of classes in which to cover more material than was humanly possible. Parents and teachers, moreover, requested the inclusion of additional subjects: other denominations, comparative religion, the saints of the church, the church seasons, etc. Parents also wanted to know what we were teaching about drugs and sex, topics which the teachers weren't clamoring to teach.

Faced with such wide demands, our priority was to address the biblical material. We attempted to familiarize the students with "The Story" of the Christian faith while at the same time inviting students to become involved with the material from their contemporary perspective. The discussion of ethics in the eighth grade class had more to do with honesty and sobriety, and less to do with sex (that is, when the adults were present). Even discussions of biblical material avoided the topic of sex for the most part. So, for example, lessons on the creation story focused on the apparent conflict between theories of creation and those of evolution, rather than on the theological significance of the relationship between Adam and Eve.

Sexuality: A Divine Gift

Several years ago the Education office at the Episcopal Church Center attempted to provide a curricular resource for parishes on sex and sexuality. The publication, *Sexuality: A Divine Gift*, proved to be extremely controversial, primarily because it was interpreted as an apology for homosexuality. I have reflected on my own experience with the curriculum at St. James' and on the failure of this national level church publication. This has convinced me that our catechetical failings have less to do with the specifics of sex and sexuality and more to do with who we are as the Body of Christ, the church.

Episcopalians know quite clearly what they *don't* want the church to be: They do not want the church to be their moral guardian or conscience. They may want the church to *teach* their children to be moral, but they don't want the church to hold adults accountable to that same teaching.

Episcopalians fear judgmentalism above all else. In an effort to be an inclusive church, we have declared that there will be no "outcasts." Even though there are "Disciplinary Rubrics" in the " Additional Directions" section of the *Book of Common Prayer* following the service of Holy Eucharist, it is difficult to imagine them actually ever being used. Of course, what comes immediately to mind when we think of a "notoriously evil life" are sexual sins like adultery, when in fact the rubrics pay closer attention to hatred between members of the congregation and to wrong doings against one's neighbor.

As offensive as we may find the idea of withholding communion from anyone for a "notoriously evil life," the rubrics nevertheless identify the central issue of being members of the Body of Christ. As the rubrics illustrate, Christians are called to live lives that reflect the life and teaching of Christ, for whom Christians are named. And so, the Body of Christ is to be marked by its love for God and one another, by repentance and forgiveness.

Adopting a single biblical paradigm as normative is always dangerous, because doing so reduces a rich witness of diversity to a single message. For example, the recent adoption of liberation themes as the paradigm for the church's life and witness has resulted in the dismissal of notions of judgment or repentance. Nevertheless, our attempts at moral education in the church will continue to fail until we adopt the baptismal promise that we will "proclaim by word and example the Good News of God in Christ" as the paradigm for church life. St. Paul says that he has been "set apart for the gospel of God" (Romans 1:1). Like Paul, those who have been baptized into the life and death of our Lord Jesus Christ have been set apart for the gospel of God, called to proclaim the Good News by word and example.

> *Traditionally, rather than being "set apart," Episcopalians have been very much a part of society's political and social structures.*

In addition to fearing judgmentalism, Episcopalians fear sectarianism. Traditionally, rather than being "set apart," Episcopalians have been very much a part of society's political and social structures. The current discussions about sexuality in the church reflect this debate: Should we flow with cultural tides and redefine what is morally permissible for Christians, or should we maintain the traditional teaching, even if doing so puts us in conflict with the larger culture? Elsewhere in this publication David A. Scott makes a strong and persuasive argument for maintaining traditional sexual ethics. I think that most parishioners in most Episcopal pews would agree with his conclusions. Nevertheless, although it seems good to most of us to live "moral" lives, we do not want to be judgmental of the way others live.

What is missing, however, is that deep conviction that by virtue of our baptism as Christians we are called to live lives that reflect our new life in Christ. This notion of being a people "set apart" was as true for God's people, Israel, as it is for God's people, the church. A number of biblical images illustrate this: the city built on a hill, the light of the world, the Body of Christ, and so forth. To be "set apart" as God's people does not imply exclusion or judgmentalism, but repentance, justification by faith, and sanctification.

> *Until the adult members of our congregation understand that being Christian means being . . . "set apart" from much of our society's values, we cannot expect our children to understand it either.*

This is the catechetical task facing our church—a task that actually needs to begin with the adult members of our congregations. What is at stake is our self-understanding as Christians. Until the adult members of our congregation understand that being Christian means being different and "set apart" from much of our society's values, we cannot expect our children to understand it either. We tell our children to "Just Say No" to drugs, alcohol, and other-than-safe sex, while we hesitate to say the same thing to ourselves about alcohol, financial dishonesty, extramarital relations, and such.

Young people in our society receive many mixed messages. For example, in a recent interview about the distribution of condoms in public schools, a Baptist pastor said he opposed distribution because it shortchanged young people. It didn't give them an opportunity to say no. He said he wanted to believe in the capacity of youth to provide such an answer, in their own moral strength and integrity. When basketball star Magic Johnson first announced that he had contracted the HIV virus, his message to the country's young people was that he should have practiced safe sex. Only later did he say he should have been abstinent.

My husband and I have a two-year-old daughter, and at times we tremble about the world she is growing up in. Sometimes we wish we could take her to a remote island and educate her at a home school to protect her from society's ills. But we know that such protection and isolation are impossible. What we need to do is to help equip her with the resources that she will need to live a full, rich, healthy life. Part of that task will be painful for all three of us, because it will mean *our* saying no to what everyone else is supposedly doing. One of the greatest challenges parents face is the temptation to give in to pressures that result from their children's exposure to the behavior of others outside the family. Parents may object to Nintendo, but buy it because their children play it at a friend's house. Other parents may supply beer for a party, reasoning that teenage drinking is unavoidable and their children might as well drink under their supervision in their own home.

No matter how strong our convictions, however, we know we cannot do what needs to be done for our daughter by ourselves. The baptismal service in the *Book of Common Prayer* asserts that we should proclaim the Good News of God in Christ by word and deed. It assumes that this cannot be done alone. Baptismal sponsors, the other members of the Body of Christ, and the power of the Holy Spirit are needed.

If the church is to provide a moral education for its members, it needs to be a supportive and accountable community as well. If the church essentially only occupies one to two hours a week of our time, then it is impossible either to transmit the Christian faith or to provide any sort of moral education to the adults and children in our congregations. The church must reclaim a dominant place in its members' spiritual, communal, and social lives. It is only possible to provide a moral education for adults and children if those individuals find reasons to gather after school, in the afternoon, and in the evening—for prayer, Bible study, support, fellowship, and entertainment.

A Community of Character

Stanley Hauerwas suggests that the church is meant to be a "Community of Character." In his book of that title he attempts to "reassert the social significance of the church as a distinct society with an integrity peculiar to itself." His goal is to "help Christians rediscover that their most important social task is nothing less than to be a community capable of hearing the story of God we find in the scripture and living in a manner that is faithful to that story."[206] The church can significantly form the lives of its members only if it is that kind of distinct society.

I wish that I could design a church school curriculum that would address the complex issues surrounding sexuality and would halt the increasing numbers of sexually active teenagers. I wish I could share success stories from St. James' or say that in retrospect I would have designed a completely different Christian Education program. But given the available 26 or 27 weeks of 30 to 45 minute class sessions I think that transmitting the biblical story is still the priority for catechesis.

What I *would* do differently, however, would be to prepare the teachers to talk about the theological significance of relationships. I would have welcomed such a publication as this, which provided a resource for discussing traditional sexual ethics, in preparing the teachers for that task. Were I in a parish doing youth group ministry, I would also include discussions in youth meetings about relationships between men and women, and between friends.

The challenge facing us, however, cannot be met by one parish priest or parent. It is the challenge of reclaiming a vision of the church as a "Community of Character," the Body of Christ in which we proclaim "by word and example the Good News of God in Christ." We are called primarily to *be* a wholesome example, and then to teach it.

CHAPTER
11

Study Guide

Mary M. Hays

The following study questions are provided for those who would like to use this text for parish discussion groups. The questions are grouped together by chapter headings.

Chapter 1
On Being Young and Single: A Challenge to the Church

1. According to Craycraft, what things make it difficult to be a single nineteen-year-old Christian? What things can you add to her list?

2. How does the author describe the differences between our culture's understanding of appropriate sexual behavior and God's design?

3. In what ways does our culture hinder (and/or help) those who are *not* young and single to live a faithful Christian life with regards to their sexuality? Are young adults the only ones who look to the church for guidance on questions of sexual morality?

4. Craycraft challenges the church "to start taking seriously its call to discipleship." In what specific ways can the church do this? How can your parish support and challenge its young people? Name one specific way you could help someone like the author.

5. What is one way Craycraft challenges or encourages you as you seek to be a faithful Christian?

Chapter 2
The Bible and Sexual Ethics

1. According to this author, what does the Old Testament say about sexual behavior? What does it affirm? What does it condemn?

2. According to this chapter, the New Testament recognizes only two forms of sexual behavior as appropriate for Christians: monogamous heterosexual marriage and celibacy. List the particular passages and/or points that support this declaration.

3. How would you summarize in a phrase or two the Bible's perspective on sexual behavior?

4. The authors maintain that Anglicans are called to base their lives first and foremost on the teachings of Scripture.

   a. What are the emotional, social, psychological, and spiritual implications of being faithful to the Scripture's teaching in the area of sexual behavior?

   b. In what specific ways can your parish support those who want to lead lives faithful to biblical standards of sexual behavior?

   c. What one thing could you do to help a fellow Christian live faithfully in this area?

   d. What help would you need from individuals or from your parish as a whole to live a life shaped by the teaching of Scripture?

Chapter 3
Human Sexuality and the Fathers of the Church

1. Trigg speaks of the patristic period as univocal on the subject of sexual behavior. What evidence does he cite for his claim? You may make a chart like the one at the top of the next page.

Patristic Author	Message

2. Trigg challenges those who read patristic authors as being supportive of homosexuality. Describe the basis for his challenge.

3. Anglicans see *tradition* as the second supporting strand of ethical decision-making. In light of Trigg's description of the earliest tradition, what should our response be? In other words, how does a univocal patristic tradition affect our understanding of sexual norms?

4. Describe how making conformity to God's will a greater priority than self-fulfillment might affect sexual behavior in this culture. What things would be the same? What things would change? What would happen if you and other Christians around you stressed obedience over self-fulfillment?

Chapter 4
Sexual Norms in the Medieval Church

1. Tell one thing you learned from this chapter—one fact, tidbit, or surprise.

2. How did the medieval church cope with people whose culture shaped them in ways contradictory to Christian morality?

3. List some of the ways that the medieval church expressed itself as pro-celibacy and pro-marriage, and as against intimate sexual behavior outside of marriage.

4. In what ways is our contemporary culture similar to medieval culture? How is it different?

5. Anglicans have traditionally based doctrine and practice on Scripture, tradition, and reason. How does the history described in this article shape our contemporary understanding of appropriate sexual behavior for Christians?

Chapter 5
Clerical Morality and Moral Discourse

1. List the things that the author tells you about the Episcopal Church's tradition regarding the expected behavior of its clergy. In what way is this understanding of behavior based on Scripture? on the ordination offices? on the Constitution and Canons?

2. Prichard says that when the Episcopal Church wants to clarify what it means by "wholesome example" or "holiness of life" it looks to General Convention. How did General Convention address alcoholism, dueling, and "amusements" in its history?

3. In what ways are the historical issues of alcoholism, dueling, and amusements similar to the current debate about sexual behavior? How are they different?

4. What position have general conventions since 1976 taken in regard to the membership of gay and lesbian persons in the Episcopal Church? What have conventions since 1979 had to say about the appropriateness of sexual relations outside of monogamous, heterosexual marriage? What steps has the Church of England taken on the same issue?

5. What problems and opportunities does the current state of this discussion in the Episcopal Church present to you and your parish?

Chapter 6
Speaking on Controversial Issues

1. McDaniel says that "Revelatory speaking is an occurrence in which speaker, hearer, and Spirit participate and in which meaning happens." According to this chapter, what is the role of the speaker in conversation? The hearer? The Spirit?

2. What happens to give our conversations with other people a "surplus of meaning"? Describe how this kind of meaning took place in a conversation you have had.

3. How can this understanding of conversation affect the way we talk about sex, sexuality, and marriage?

4. The author says that when we talk about controversial issues we should speak "with conviction and compassion while at the same time we listen and learn." What are some specific ways to do this in our conversations? What things get in the way of our having this kind of conversation on controversial issues?

Chapter 7
Homosexuality: The Behavioral Sciences and the Church

1. According to this article, what are some of the possible causes of homosexuality?

2. What is an appropriate relationship between the social sciences and Christian ethical decision-making? In light of the research described in this article, what role should Christians have in making decisions about issues that involve homosexuality?

3. In what ways do the findings of psychology seem to affirm the biblical and traditional Christian position regarding sexual behavior?

4. In what ways might these findings challenge the way that the church has understood sexual behavior?

Chapter 8
Traditional Sexual Ethics: Making a Case

1. What are the hallmarks of a traditional sexual ethic according to the author?

2. What are the underlying assumptions of a traditional Christian sexual ethic?

3. What are the characteristics of a personalist sexual ethic?

4. How did our culture provide a framework for a personalist sexual ethic to develop?

5. Scott talks about separating the private sphere from the public sphere. What are some of the implications for Christians in separating these two worlds?

6. According to Scott, what are some of the positive features of a personalist sexual ethic? What other positive features might you include?

7. How does Scott criticize the personalist sexual ethic? What other criticism do you see?

8. List the components of a sexual ethic that would take seriously the Christian's call to be faithful to God and sensitive to the culture.

9. Imagine that several newcomers ask for help in understanding your parish's view of sexual ethics. Try to write a "parish sexual ethic." Consider some or all of the following as you frame your statement:
   - What the Bible says about sexuality and sexual behavior
   - How the church has historically understood these issues
   - What the Episcopal Church currently says
   - The insights of the behavioral sciences

Chapter 9
Sexual Morality and Pastoral Care

1. Make a list of possible responses the church can make to people of non-traditional life-styles.

2. In your own words, describe the difference between an "interim suspension of judgment" and an "ultimate suspension of judgment" toward persons living non-traditional life-styles who need pastoral care.

3. Describe a response that reflects an "interim suspension of judgment" to:
   - a divorced man living with a woman he intends to marry
   - a thirty-year-old man who is about to tell his parents that he is gay
   - a pregnant teenager who doesn't know the identity of the father of her unborn child

   Consider your initial responses, how Scripture and tradition would influence your reflection and conversation, and how you would balance pastoral sensitivity with pastoral challenge.

Chapter 10
By Word and Example: The Church and Moral Education

1. List the reasons the author gives for challenging the church to take moral education seriously.

2. According to the author, why have Episcopalians had difficulty developing a helpful approach to education about sex and sexuality? What problems could you add to her list from your own experience as a Christian and a member of a parish?

3. Turner points out that any moral education must be supported by a Christian community that can articulate and live out the Good News of God in Jesus Christ. What are some of the ways a parish could speak out of its convictions about sex and sexuality? How specifically could a parish support its members as they seek to lead lives that are godly examples with regard to sexual attitudes and behaviors?

4. Describe one thing that your parish is doing to be the kind of supportive Christian community Turner describes. Name one thing that would make your parish more supportive for those seeking to lead faithful lives.

5. Tell one specific way that you could "by word and example proclaim the Good News of God in Christ" in the arena of sex and sexuality.

NOTES

Chapter Two

[1]John E. Booty, *What Makes Us Episcopalians?* (Wilton, Conn.: Morehouse-Barlow, 1982).

Richard Hooker is often credited with identifying the trio of Anglican authorities. His trio differed, however, both from the three-fold and the four-fold formulations used by contemporary Episcopalians. Hooker spoke of "what Scripture doth plainly deliver" as deserving "the first place both of credit and obedience." His second authority was "whatsoever any man can necessarily conclude by force of reason," by which he meant convictions and ideas that had the force of common consent. His third authority was "the voice of the Church," by which he meant the official pronouncements and policies of the church hierarchy. These three authorities had priority over "all inferior judgments whatsoever." See: Richard Hooker, *Of the Laws of Ecclesiastical Polity*, 5.7.2.

[2]Article VII of the Constitution, *Constitutions and Canons for the Government of the Protestant Episcopal Church in the United States of America, Otherwise Known as the Episcopal Church, Adopted in General Conventions, 1789-1988* (Revised by the Convention, 1988), 7. The declaration, which appears in each of the ordination offices, is modeled on the sixth of the Thirty-nine Articles.

[3] See Deuteronomy 5:6-21 for a parallel text of later composition.

[4] *Book of Common Prayer* (1979), 350.

[5] Leviticus 18-20 also identifies a fifth sexual practice as unacceptable—engaging in sexual intercourse during menstruation. This is, however, an objection of a different order from that to incest, adultery, homosexuality, and bestiality. The condemnation is closely related to the ceremonial prohibition against the spilling of blood, and has nothing to do with the moral question of the character and status of the participants themselves. One can also note that the punishment prescribed in Leviticus 20 is less severe than that for adultery, homosexuality, bestiality, and some forms of incest.

Sexual intercourse during menstruation is not explicitly discussed in the New Testament. The story of Jesus' encounter with the woman who had suffered hemorrhages for 12 years (Matthew 9:20-22; Mark 5:25-34; Luke 8:43-48) does indicate, however, that New Testament authors were doing some rethinking of the Old Testament prohibitions about contact with blood.

[6] The teaching of the New Testament would mitigate the excessive punishments mandated in Leviticus 20, but would by no means abrogate the commandments themselves.

[7] William Countryman, *Dirt, Greed, and Sex* (Philadelphia: Fortress, 1988), 73.

[8] Gerhard Kittel and Gerhard Friedrich, *Theological Dictionary of the New Testament*, 10 vols. (Grand Rapids: Wm. B. Eerdmans, 1964-76), 6:590.

[9] See John Boswell, *Christianity, Social Tolerance, and Homosexuality: Gay People in Western Europe from the Beginning of the Christian Era to the Fourteenth Century* (Chicago: University of Chicago Press, 1980), 108.

[10] See Richard B. Hays, "Relations Natural and Unnatural: A Response to John Boswell's Exegesis of Romans 1," *The Journal of Religious Ethics* 14 (Spring 1986):192-194 and Boswell, *Christianity, Social Tolerance, and Homosexuality*, 109.

[11] Boswell, *Christianity, Social Tolerance, and Homosexuality*, 108.

[12] This also seems to have been the point in the two passages in Genesis which record sexual relations between humans and angels.

In one case (Genesis 6:2) the relations are heterosexual, in the other (Genesis 19:1-11), homosexual. Neither case, however, conforms to the pattern of human male and female heterosexual marriage, and both incur divine punishment. Those who seek to identify lack of hospitality to strangers as the major sin in Genesis 19 have missed the point. It is not that humans committed one particular act that was sinful, but rather that humanity's rebellion against God led to a disorder in which all kinds of sin abound. Fratricide, estrangement from brute creation, miscommunication, and sexual irregularities are all results of and signs of that rebellion.

[13]Boswell, *Christianity, Social Tolerance, and Homosexuality,* 109.

[14]Hays, "Relations Natural and Unnatural," 200-01.

[15]Ibid., 191.

[16]Boswell, *Christianity, Social Tolerance, and Homosexuality,* 106-08; Countryman, *Dirt, Greed, and Sex,* 117-20.

[17]Hans Conzelmann, *1 Corinthians: A Commentary on the First Epistle to the Corinthians,* trans. James W. Leitch, ed. George W. MacRae (Philadelphia: Fortress, Hermeneia series, [1975]), 106.

[18]*Encyclopedia of Early Christianity* (New York: Garland Publishing, 1990), s.v. "Homosexuality" by David F. Wright.

[19]Countryman, *Dirt, Greed and Sex,* 237.

Chapter Three

[20]Gregory of Nazianzus, *Orationes,* 9.8.

[21]Augustine, *De Bono Conjugali,* 8.8.

[22]On this matter see Frans Van der Meer, *Augustine the Bishop* (London: Sheed and Ward, 1961), 180-90.

[23]Peter Brown, *The Body and Society: Men, Women, and Sexual Renunciation in Early Christianity,* (New York: Columbia University Press, 1988).

[24]K.J. Dover, *Greek Homosexuality* (Cambridge: Harvard University Press, 1978).

[25]William L. Peterson, "The Study of 'Homosexuality' in Patristic Sources," *Studia Patristica* 20 (1989):285.

[26] Among works from the second century alone, see *Didache* 2.2; *Ps. Barnabas* 10; Justin, *Dialogus* 95; and Tatian, *Cohortatio* 8.1 for *paidophthoria* and Theophilus, *Ad Autolycum* 1.2 and 14 for *arsenokoitia*. For other examples of Patristic condemnations of homosexual behavior, see *Dictionary of Early Christianity*, s.v. "Homosexuality" by David F. Wright.

[27] Eusebius, *Praeparatio Evangelica*, 13.20.7.

[28] See John Chrysostom, *Hom. in Gen.* 43.3-4 and Ps.-Macarius, *Hom.* 4.22.

[29] *Const. Ap.*, 6.28.1-3.

[30] John Boswell, *Christianity, Social Tolerance, and Homosexuality: Gay People in Western Europe from the Beginning of the Christian Era to the Fourteenth Century* (Chicago: University of Chicago Press, 1980), 46.

[31] Ibid., 48.

[32] Ibid., 135.

[33] Augustine, *Sermones*, 280.1.

[34] Boswell, *Christianity, Social Tolerance, and Homosexuality*, 135. For further discussion of this passage, see Joseph W. Trigg, "What do the Church Fathers Have to Tell Us About Sex?" in *ATR* 74 (1992): 18-24.

[35] See Peter Brown, *Augustine of Hippo* (Berkeley: University of California Press, 1969), 200-02.

[36] Boswell, *Christianity, Social Tolerance, and Homosexuality*, 133.

[37] Peter Brown, *The Cult of the Saints* (Chicago: The University of Chicago Press, 1981), 53-67.

[38] Peterson, "Study of Homosexuality," 288.

Chapter Four

[39] Lawrence Stone, *The Family, Sex, and Marriage in England 1500-1800* (London, 1977), ch.2. The theory that the prohibition of fornication was suited to societies in which people married at puberty, but not to modern adolescence, receives no support at all from current demographic studies of the middle ages, in which the age of marriage appears to have been roughly similar to that in modern societies.

[40]Sexual behavior, of course, was only one of the many arenas for this process. The same sort of dialectic took place over war and peace, criminal trials, banking, healing—indeed virtually every element of pre-modern life.

[41]E.g. the 12th c. dictum of Gratian, summarizing canonical evidence: "Fornicatio licet videatur esse genus cuiuslibet illiciti coitus, qui fit extra uxorem legitimam . . . ." (*Decretum,* 2a pars, causa xxxv, q.1, in Emil Friedberg, ed., *Corpus Iuris Canonici* [Leipzig, 1876]).

[42]As a result, during the middle ages marriage could never pretend to be spiritually absolute, or necessary for all. The higher status then accorded to celibacy placed an eschatological question mark after marriage. That could result in consigning married people to a sort of second-class citizenship, but could also limit the social imperialism of the married state. The Reformation fiercely criticized the medieval church for outlawing clerical marriage and for fomenting works-righteousness in the form of voluntary celibacy. It praised marriage as an estate established by God. Yet all of the Reformers acknowledged the biblical basis of celibacy and (in principle) its utility. By destroying monasteries, however, they set in motion a long process by which successful bourgeois marriage and social normality came to seem synonymous.

[43]E.g. the formal legal definition of Gratian, drawn from Justinian through Peter Lombard: "Sunt enim nuptiae sive matrimonium viri mulierisque individuam vitae consuetudinem retinens" ("Marriage is the union of a man and a woman, preserving an indivisible relationship"). Gratian, *Decretum* 2a pars, causa xxvii, q.2, 1 pars.

[44]See Jean Leclercq, *Monks on Marriage: A Twelfth Century View* (New York: Seabury Press, 1981); and *Monks and Love in Twelfth-century France: Psycho-Historical Essays* (Oxford: Clarendon Press, 1979).

[45]Scholastic theologians analyzed the Old Testament cases seeming to prove the contrary, for example, those in which patriarchs had children by slave women. Generally they followed Augustine in arguing that the patriarchs (1) had lived under a different dispensation, and (2) that God had directly commanded them to do what they did. Thus a few of them (chiefly "nominalists") acknowledged the speculative possibility that God could alter the list of prohibited acts, or

that God could command any believer to perform a certain action and thus render right something which otherwise would be wrong. This analytical exploration had no influence on pastoral teaching, any more than physicists' speculation on alternative universes with different physical laws influences the way they teach their children to drive cars.

[46]Thomas Aquinas, *Summa Theologiae*, 2da, 2dae, q.154.

[47]Note the contrast between the prayers, "Deus qui tam excellenti mysterio" and the conclusion of "Deus per quem mulier," in J. Wickham Legg, ed., *Sarum Missal* (Oxford, 1916), 417. There is in fact a rich diversity of theme and reference in all the rites: see the marriage orders published in Edmund Martène, *De Antiquis Ecclesiae Ritibus* (Rotomagi, 1700), Liber I, caput IX, article v.

[48]Pierre J. Payer, *Sex and the Penitentials: the Development of a Sexual Code 550-1150* (Toronto: University of Toronto Press, 1984), 29ff. In Appendix D, Payer refutes certain of the claims made by John Boswell about early medieval homosexuality in Boswell's influential but often highly misleading study, *Christianity, Social Tolerance, and Homosexuality* (Chicago: University of Chicago Press, 1980).

[49]Thomas Aquinas, *Summa Theologiae*, 2da, 2dae, q.154, art.2.

[50]See especially the Penitential of Adamnan in Ludwig Bieler, ed., *The Irish Penitentials* (Dublin, 1975).

[51]Peter Damian, *Book of Gomorrah: an Eleventh-Century Treatise against Clerical Homosexual Practices*, ed. Pierre J. Payer (Waterloo, Ont.: Wilfrid Laurier University Press, 1982).

[52]There is a good introduction to these rites in A.G. Martimort, ed., *Eglise en Prière* (Paris, 1961). See W. G. Henderson, ed., *Liber Pontificalis Chr. Bainbridge Archiep. Eboracensis*, Surtees Society vol. LXI (Durham, 1875), 81ff, 154ff.

[53]Surveyed by Kenneth Stevenson, *Nuptial Blessing. A Study of Christian Marriage Rites*, Alcuin Club Collections No. 64 (London, 1982), and by P. Jounel in Martimort, *Eglise en Prière*, 596ff.

[54]References to Genesis 1 and 2 are almost universal. See the widely used prayer, "Deus per quem mulier," conveniently found in Legg, ed., *Sarum Missal*, 417.

[55]See, for example, the lovely episcopal benediction in Henderson, ed., *Liber Pontificalis Chr. Bainbridge*, 182.

[56]This too was variously explained, often by asserting that flesh which had been blessed in the previous marriage required no further blessing, and would draw the new husband or wife into it. See, for example, the York liturgies.

[57]See for example Martène, *De Antiquis Ecclesiae Ritibus*, who prints sixteen medieval marriage orders, and W. G. Henderson, ed., *Manuale et Processionale ad usum . . . ecclesiae Eboracensis*, Surtees Society vol. LXIII (Durham, 1875), who prints a dozen more.

[58]For details of Professor Boswell's claim see Susan E. Pierce, "Same-sex marriage is nothing new," *Witness* 71 (October 1988). Boswell spoke in October of 1988 to Integrity on the subject, "A Thousand Years of the Church Blessing Lesbian and Gay Relationships—It's Nothing New." According to Pierce's account, Boswell had discovered a same-sex marriage ceremony widely represented in medieval manuscripts. This finding, the *Witness* story suggested, was the result of his research for a book due to be published from Pantheon Press in February, 1989. On March 27, 1991, my colleague, Dr. Robert Prichard, spoke with Pantheon Press and with Prof. Boswell's secretary, to discover if the relevant texts or studies were yet in print. Pantheon Press had no record of any plans for a Boswell book on homosexual liturgies. Prof. Boswell's secretary, after conferring with him, reported that he had not published any preliminary articles on the subject and did not have a publisher for the project.

[59]Martène, *De Antiquis Ecclesiae Ritibus*, ordo XIV. My translation.

[60]The form in the York Manual declares that the witnesses "come here to couple and knit these two bodies together, that is to say of this man and this woman, that they be from this time forth but one body and two souls in the faith and law of God and of Holy Church, for to deserve everlasting life, whatsoever(!) they have done here before." It goes on to discuss the bans, and to assert in very strong terms the importance of public marriage so as to avoid relationships which are either covers for fornication (i.e. not real marriages, since mutual consent to real marriage has not occurred) or permit the separation of those truly married (i.e. where such consent has oc-

curred but, because secret, may be forgotten or ignored). Henderson, ed., *Manuale et Processionale... Eccl. Eboracensis*, 24-27. It was not necessary to obtain a public ecclesial blessing, however, for a marriage to be canonically valid. In England, the clear and uncoerced consent of an unhindered man and an unhindered woman was sufficient by itself to create a canonically valid marriage. Gratian, *Decretum*, causa XXVII, q.2, 1 pars.

[61]W.G. Henderson, ed., *Missale ad usum... ecclesiae Herfordensis* (1874; reprint, Farnborough: 1968), 443.

[62]As one piece of anecdotal evidence, I have been studying the primary sources of the medieval Latin church and society for twenty-five years, and have never found a single reference to the church's blessing of a relationship including sexual acts, except that of life-long marriage between man and woman.

[63]John McNeill and Helen Gamer, *Medieval Handbooks of Penance* (New York, 1938); Ludwig Bieler, ed., *Irish Penitentials*; Pierre J. Payer, *Sex and the Penitentials*.

[64]Thomas Tentler, *Sin and Confession on the Eve of the Reformation* (Princeton: Princeton University Press, 1977).

Chapter Five

[65]*Book of Common Prayer* (1979), 513, 526, 538. See Chapter Two of this book for a discussion of Biblical attitudes toward gay and lesbian behavior.

[66]In order to conform 1 Timothy 3 to the three orders of the ministry, *The Great Bible* had translated *diakonos* in verse eight as "minister," but in verses twelve and thirteen as "deacon." The *King James Bible* abandoned this convention, and the revisers in 1662 accordingly dropped the lesson from the ordination of priests.

[67]*Book of Common Prayer* (1979), 513, 526, 538.

[68]*The First and Second Prayer Books of Edward VI* (London: Dent, Everyman's Library, 1968), 439.

[69]*Book of Common Prayer* (1979), 526, 538.

[70]*First and Second Prayer Books*, 439, 453.

[71]*The First and Second Prayer Books*, 447, 456, 461. The words "wholesome example," absent in the examination of candidates to

the episcopate, did appear in the ordination of bishops in the closing prayer.

[72]*Book of Common Prayer* (1928), 531, 537, 559.

[73]*Book of Common Prayer* (1979), 523, 535, 547.

[74]*Constitution and Canons for the Government of the Protestant Episcopal Church in the United States of America Otherwise Known as the Episcopal Church, Adopted in General Conventions, 1789-1988* (revised for the Convention, 1988), 69-70.

The testimonial's language concerning morality has changed only slightly since 1789. Initially the canon required a testimonial indicating that any candidate for ordination "hath lived piously, soberly, and honestly." In 1904 this formula was altered to read "hath lived a sober, honest, and godly life."

The General Convention of 1832 limited the time period covered by the testimonial to "the space of three years last past," a provision that remains in the current canon.

[75]Edward Cardwell, ed., *Synodalia: a Collection of Articles of Religion, Canons, and Proceedings of Convocations in the Providence of Canterbury from the Year 1547 to the Year 1717,* 2 vols. (Oxford: Oxford University Press, 1842; Farborough, Hants.: Gregg Press, 1966), 2:290.

[76]*Canons for the Government of the Protestant Episcopal Church in the Unites States of America* (New York: Protestant Episcopal Press. 1832), 27.

[77]Edwin Augustine White and Jack A. Dykman, *Annotated Constitution and Canons for the Government of the Protestant Episcopal Church in the United States of American, Otherwise Known as the Episcopal Church, Adopted in General Conventions, 1789-1979,* 2 vols. (New York: Seabury, 1982-85), 2:966.

[78]This tradition is very different from that in some other denominations, most notably the Roman Catholic Church. A meeting of an Episcopal and a Roman Catholic seminary faculty several years ago illustrated that basic difference. The topic was the spiritual nurture of seminary students. A speaker from the Episcopal seminary briefly alluded to the ordination offices' inquiry into faithfulness in prayer and reading of Scripture (*Book of Common Prayer* [1979], 544). The speaker then, in good common law tradition, described the spiritual

disciplines tried in the past at the Episcopal institution, identified the most profitable, and outlined those currently in use. The Roman Catholic presenter, in good Roman law tradition, identified a Vatican statement on spiritual nurture of students and described it at great length without once referring to actual practice. For the Episcopalian, practice and regulation interacted in a way that it did not for the Roman Catholic.

[79]During the nineteenth century Episcopal courts made precisely this point in both the trial of Joseph Trapnall of Maryland (1847) and Bishop Benjamin Boswell Smith of Kentucky. Both had argued that the offenses for which they were charged were not specifically named in the canons. The courts ruled that specific infractions against religion and morals need not be named. See Edwin Augustin White, *Constitution and Canons for the Government of the Protestant Episcopal Church in the United States of America, Adopted in General Conventions, 1789-1922, Annotated etc.* (New York: Edwin S. Gorham, 1924), 566-67.

Jackson A. Dykman, who prepared new editions of White's commentary on the canons in 1954 and again in 1982-5, was apparently convinced by the decision of the court of review of the Fifth Province in the trial of L. Peter Beebe that charges based on a breach of discipline may need to be specified in canon. Dykman does not, however, raise similar questions about moral offenses. See White and Dykman, *Annotated Constitution and Canons* (1982-85), 2:970-72.

[80]Title IV, Canon 3 provides for the creation of courts for ecclesiastical trials. In the case of presbyters and deacons, the canons direct individual dioceses to make provisions for courts and trial procedures. There is in addition a provision for a court of review chosen by the provincial synod. Although Article IX of the Constitution provides for "the establishment of Courts of Review" and for "an ultimate Court of Appeal, solely for the review of the determination of any Court of Review on questions of Doctrine, Faith, or Worship," the General Convention has never acted on the provision. There is, therefore, no national court of appeals.

The situation is somewhat different in the case of bishops. The canons provide for both a court and a court of review. The members of both courts are elected by the House of Bishops.

[81]Two factors prevent this figure from being anything more than a rough approximation of the number of trials and ecclesiastical actions. The first is the inclusion of voluntary resignations in which no crime or immorality has been alleged. This factor undoubtedly contributed to the increase in numbers in the period from 1971 to 1982. The second factor is the exclusion from this figure of trials or disciplinary actions that ended in acquittal or some decision short of deposition, removal, release, or renunciation. To some degree, however, the two factors balance one another, for the first would cause the estimate of trials and disciplinary actions to be overstated, the second, to be understated.

[82]Figures are from the Report of the Recorder of Ordinations in the *Journals of the General Convention* between 1949 and 1988. The composite triennial figures for depositions, removals (first reported in 1973), renunciations (1979), and releases (1985) are as follows: 1949-38; 1952-54; 1955-70; 1958-58; 1961-80; 1964-82; 1967-82; 1970-71; 1973-111; 1976-92; 1979-158; 1982-131; 1985-102; 1988-98.

[83]Title VI, Canon 8, section 1 specifies that before accepting a renunciation of the ministry the bishop should be "satisfied that the person so declaring is not amenable for any canonical offense, and that his renunciation of the Ministry is not occasioned by foregoing misconduct or irregularity."

A suit for deprivation of livelihood brought in the mid-1980s by a clergyman permitted to leave the ministry without trial may have caused some bishops to rethink the policy of allowing those guilty of indiscretion to renounce their orders without trial.

[84]Prior to the 1973 alteration in marriage canons, clergy were often deposed from the ministry because of divorce. Since the 1973 decision to allow remarriage in a wider number of circumstances, clergy are rarely, if ever, charged for the fact of divorce itself. In most circumstances the cause of the presentment is adultery or fornication with parishioners. Those presented for homosexual infractions are often charged with soliciting or engaging in sex in public or with child molestation.

[85]W.J. Rorabaugh, *The Alcoholic Republic* (Oxford: Oxford University Press, 1978), 8.

[86]The actual election was in 1783, before the creation of the General Convention.

[87]At the time of the initial 1785 constitution General Convention was a unicameral body. The convention of 1789 created a separate House of Bishops and adopted a revised constitution that required consent of both the House of Deputies and the House of Bishops for an episcopal consecration. The convention of 1799 revised this procedure slightly, allowing a vote by the majority of bishops and the majority of diocesan standing committees, if the General Convention were in recess. See Daniel B. Stevick, *Canon Law: a Handbook* (New York: Seabury, 1965), 105.

[88]William Stevens Perry, ed., *Journals of General Conventions of the Protestant Episcopal Church in the United States, 1785-1835*, 2 vols. (Claremont, N. H.: Claremont Manufacturing, 1874), 1:128.

[89]Cardwell, ed., *Synodalia*, 1:290.

[90]White and Dykman, *Annotated Constitution and Canons*, 2:965-66.

[91]Robert W. Prichard, *A History of the Episcopal Church* (Wilton, Conn.: Morehouse, 1991), 106-07.

[92]Perry, ed., *Journals*, 1:348.

[93]Ibid., 1:378.

[94]For an expression of disapproval in a clerical manual see Gilbert Burnet, *A Discourse of the Pastoral Care*, 14th ed. (London: Rivingtons and Cochran, 1821), 183. In 1808 the General Convention made Burnet's *Discourse* required reading for the ministry.

[95]William White, *Memoirs of the Protestant Episcopal Church in the United States of America* (New York: E.P. Dutton, 1880), 44, 425-27.

[96]The Gallup Organization, *The Spiritual Health of the Episcopal Church* (Washington, D.C.: Episcopal Parish Services, 1990), 21.

[97]*Journal of the General Convention of the Protestant Episcopal Church in the United States of America, Otherwise Known as the Episcopal Church . . . 1976* (printed for the convention, 1976), C-108.

[98]*Journal of the General Convention of the Protestant Episcopal Church in the United States of America . . . 1979* (New York: Seabury Professional Services, 1979), B-191-92.

[99]Ibid, B-97.

[100]*Journal of the General Convention of the Protestant Episcopal Church . . . 1988* (New York: Seabury Professional Services, 1988), 296-97.

[101]J. Gordon Melton, ed., *The Churches Speak on Homosexuality: Official Statements from Religious Bodies and Ecumenical Organizations* (Detroit: Gale Research, 1991), 66.

[102]Ibid., 102-03.

[103]House of Bishops of the General Synod of the Church of England, *Issues in Human Sexuality* (London: Church House Publishing, 1991), section 5.2.

[104]Ibid., section 5.4.

[105]Ibid., sections 5.5-5.22.

[106]Ibid., section 5.15.

[107]"Statement by the Presiding Bishop and Council of Advice," February 20, 1990.

[108]James Solheim and Jeffrey Penn, "Bishops Narrowly Vote to 'Disassociate' from Homosexual Ordination in Newark," *Episcopal News Service* (26 September 1990): 19.

[109]Standing Commission on Human Affairs, "Report of the Commission with Resolutions," *The Blue Book* (New York: Episcopal Church, 1991), 204.

[110]*Virginia Episcopalian* 99 (May 1991): 22.

[111]"Sexuality Debated at General Convention: Conservative Views Receive Setback," *The Living Church* 203 (4 August 1991): 6.

[112]In the House of Deputies, a majority of dioceses in both orders must vote for a resolution in order for it to pass.

[113]*Episcopal Life* 2 (August 1991): 6.

[114]Jerry Hames, "Compromise Reached on Sexuality," *Episcopal Life* 2 (August 1991):1 and 6.

Chapter Six

[115]See John Shelby Spong, *Rescuing the Bible from Fundamentalism* (San Francisco: Harper, 1991) for an example of this style of argumentation.

[116]Vincent of Lerins was the author of the often repeated definition for catholicity: " 'that which has been believed everywhere, always and by all'" (Vincent of Lerins quoted by John Macquarrie, *Principles of Christian Theology* [New York: Charles Scribner's Sons, 1966], 11.). It is a definition that draws attention to the relationship between the truth of a proposition and the community's assent to that proposition.

[117]John Henry Newman, *An Essay on the Development of Christian Doctrine* (New York: D. Appleton & Company, 1845).

[118]Newman outlined seven criteria by which to distinguish the development of doctrine from its corruption (type versus variation; continuity versus alteration; unitive power of assimilation versus instability; intimations of future versus infidelity; sequence versus contradiction; conservative versus reverse order; duration versus energetic and transitory). These functioned by way of the juxtaposition of opposites.

That each of these principles is common to many subjects, not just Christian doctrine, is readily apparent. Adherence to type did not mean dogmatic refusal to change, but neither did it mean an unrestricted variation to the point of the dissolution of type. Indeed, change according to principles was the governing principle behind each of these antithetical pairs. And that is a useful standard in a variety of situations. Likewise, the conservative principle did not mean "circling the wagons," much less going backward. Rather, it carried to the future the preservative qualities of the past.

[119]See particularly Martin Heidegger, *Being and Time*, trans. John Macquarrie and Edward Robinson (London: SCM Press, 1962) and *On the Way to Language*, trans. Peter D. Hertz (New York: Harper & Row, 1971).

[120]Calvin O. Schrag, *Communicative Praxis and the Space of Subjectivity* (Bloomington: Indiana University Press, 1986).

[121]Paul Ricoeur, in *Paul Ricoeur: Hermeneutics and the Human Sciences*, ed. and trans. John B. Thompson (Cambridge: Cambridge

University Press, 1981).

[122]John Stewart, "Dimension of Dialogue in Gadamer's Theory and Practice," paper presented to the "Multiple Conceptions of Dialogue," panel, Speech Communication Association Convention, November 1986, 9.

[123]John Stewart, "Speech and Human Being: A Complement to Semiotics," *Quarterly Journal of Speech* 72 (1986): 55-73.

[124]Hans-Georg Gadamer quoted in Richard E. Palmer, *Hermeneutics* (Evanston: Northwestern University Press, 1969), 208.

[125]Palmer, *Hermeneutics*, 188.

[126]Barbara Warnick, "A Ricoeurian Approach to Rhetorical Criticism," a paper to the Speech Communication Association Convention, November 1986, 11.

[127]Palmer, *Hermeneutics*, 215.

[128]Palmer, *Hermeneutics*, 212.

[129]Palmer, *Hermeneutics*, 188.

[130]John Stewart, ed., *Bridges, Not Walls* (New York: Random House, 1986), 183.

[131]John Stewart, "Martin Buber's Central Insight: Implications for his Philosophy of Dialogue," *Dialogue — An Interdisciplinary Approach*, ed. Marcelo Dascal (Amsterdam: John Benjamins Publishing Co., 1985), 325.

[132]Richard Lischer, *A Theology of Preaching* (Nashville: Abingdon, 1981), 96.

[133]Sallie McFague, *Metaphorical Theology* (Philadelphia: Fortress Press, 1982), 2.

[134]Parker J. Palmer, *To Know As We Are Known* (San Francisco: Harper & Row, 1983), 43.

[135]McFague, *Metaphorical Theology*, 165.

Chapter Seven

[136]This article is reprinted with permission from the *Journal of Psychology and Theology* 17 (1989):213-25. Dr. William F. Hunter is the *Journal*'s Editor. The editorial offices are located at 13800 Biola Lane, La Miranda, California 90639.

The first author presented an earlier version of this article on October 17, 1987, at the conference on "Homosexuality and the Church," sponsored by the Midwest region of the United Methodist Church, in Downers Grove, Illinois. A condensed form of this earlier version appeared in *Christianity Today* 33 (August 18, 1989): 26-29. Requests for reprints should be sent to Stanton L. Jones, Ph.D., Department of Psychology, Wheaton College, Wheaton, Illinois 60187.

[137]H.Richard Niebuhr, *Christ and Culture* (New York: Harper & Row, 1951).

[138]E. Brooks Holifield, *A History of Pastoral Care in America* (Nashville: Abingdon, 1983).

[139]R. Bayer, *Homosexuality and American Psychiatry: The Politics of Diagnosis* (New York: Basic, 1981), 167.

[140]Ibid.

[141]Ibid.

[142]J. Bieber. "A Discussion of Homosexuality: The Ethical Challenge," *Journal of Consulting and Clinical Psychology* 44 (1976):163-66. M. Hunt, *Sexual Behavior in the 1970's* (Chicago: Playboy, 1974).

[143]A.C. Kinsey, W.B. Pomeroy, and C.E. Martin, *Sexual Behavior in the Human Male* (Philadelphia: W.B. Saunders, 1948).

[144]Ibid.

[145]Ibid., 625, 650 [emphasis in original].

[146]A.C. Pomeroy cited in Hunt, *Sexual Behavior*, 308.

[147]Hunt, *Sexual Behavior*, 308.

[148]M. Ross, J. Paulson and O. Stalstrom, "Homosexuality and Mental Health," *Journal of Homosexuality* 15 (1988): 131-52.

[149]A.P. Bell and M.S. Weinberg, *Homosexualities: A Study of Diversity among Men and Women* (New York: Simon and Schuster, 1978), 207.

[150]R. Kus, "Alcohol and the Non-acceptance of Gay Self," *Journal of Homosexuality* 15 (1988): 25-42.

[151]E. Pattison and J. Kahan, "The Deliberate Self-harm Syndrome," *American Journal of Psychiatry* 137 (1983): 867-72.

[152]Bell and Weinberg, *Homosexualities*, 346.

[153]Ibid., 308.

[154]E.g., see the way D. P. McWhirter and A. M. Mattison, ("Treatment of Sexual Dysfunction in Homosexual Male Couples," in S.R. Leiblum and L.A. Pervin, eds. *Principles and Practices of Sex Therapy* [New York: Guilford, 1980], 321-45.), and J. Prochaska and J. Prochaska ("Twentieth Century Trends in Marriage and Marital Therapy," in T. Paolino and B. McCrady, eds., *Marriage and Marital Therapy* [New York: Brunner/Mazel, 1978], 1-24.) treated relational stability.

[155]E. Moberly, *Psychogenesis: The Early Development of Gender Identity* (London: Routledge and Kegan Paul, 1983).

[156]J. Davis and T. Smith, *General Social Survey (1972-1984): Cumulative Data* (New Haven, Conn.: Yale University Press, 1984).

[157]J. S. Nevid, "Exposure to Homoerotic Stimuli: Effects on Attitudes and Affects of Heterosexual Viewers," *The Journal of Social Psychology* 119 (1983): 249-55.

[158]Ibid., 254.

[159]Allen Bergin, "Three Contributions of a Spiritual Perspective to Psychotherapy and Behavioral Change," in W. Miller and J. Martin, eds., *Behavioral Therapy and Religion: Integrating Spiritual and Behavioral Approaches to Change* (Newbury Park, Ca.: Sage, 1988), 25-36.

[160]Ibid., 32.

[161]F. Kallman, "Comparative Twin Study on the Genetic Aspects of Male Homosexuality," *Journal of Nervous and Mental Disease* 115 (1952): 137-59.

[162]F. Kallman cited in A. Cooper, "The Aetiology of Homosexuality," in B. Loraine, ed. *Understanding Homosexuality* (New York: American Elsevier, 1974), 1-24.

[163]J. Money, "Genetic and Chromosomal Aspects of Homosexual Etiology," in Judd Marmor, ed., *Homosexual Behavior: A Modern Reappraisal* (New York: Basic, 1980), 69-70.

[164]Ibid.

[165]L. Ellis and A. Ames, "Neurohormonal Functioning and Sexual Orientation: A Theory of Homosexuality-Heterosexuality, "*Psychological Bulletin* 101 (1987): 233-58.

[166]Ibid., 252.

[167]J. Money, "Sin, Sickness, or Status? Homosexual Gender Identity and Psychoneuroendocrinology," *American Psychologist* 42 (1987):398.

[168]R. Friedman, *Male Homosexuality* (New Haven: Yale University Press, 1988); G. Tourney, "Hormones and Homosexuality," in Marmor, ed., *Homosexual Behavior*, 41-58.

[169]J. Bieber, "A Discussion of Homosexuality," 164.

[170]C. Wolff, *Love Between Women* (New York: Harper & Row, 1971).

[171]Marmor, ed., *Homosexual Behavior*, 10.

[172]C. Socarides, *Homosexuality* (New York: Jason Aronson, 1978); E. Moberly, *Psychogenesis: The Early Development of Gender Identity* (London: Routledge and Kegan Paul, 1983).

[173]R. Friedman, "The Psychoanalytic Model of Male Homosexuality: A Historical and Theoretical Critique," *The Psychoanalytic Review* 73 (1986): 79-115; R. Friedman, *Male Homosexuality* (New Haven: Yale University Press, 1988).

[174]R. Green, *The 'Sissy Boy' Syndrome and the Development of Homosexuality*, (New Haven: Yale University Press, 1987).

[175]M. Storms, "A Theory of Erotic Orientation Development," *Psychological Review* 88 (1981): 340-53.

[176]R. Denniston, "Ambisexuality in Animals," in Marmor, ed., *Homosexual Behavior*, 38-39.

[177]P. Tyler, "Homosexual Behavior in Animals," in K. Howells, ed., *The Psychology of Sexual Diversity* (New York: Basil Blackwell, 1984).

[178]J. Carrier, "Homosexual Behavior in Cross-cultural Perspective," in Marmor, ed., *Homosexual Behavior*, 59-74; W. Masters, V. Johnson and R. Kolodny, *Human Sexuality*, 2d. ed. (Boston: Little, Brown & Co., 1985).

[179]R. Stoller and G. Herdt, "Theories of Origin of Male Homosexuality: A Cross-cultural Look," *Archives of General Psychiatry* 42 (1985): 399-404.

[180]J. Carrier, "Homosexual Behavior in Cross-cultural Perspective," in Marmor, ed. *Homosexual Behavior*, 59-74.

[181]J. Money, "Genetic and Chromosomal Aspects of Homosexual Etiology," 59-74; J. Money, "Sin, Sickness, or Status?" 384-99.

[182]Bieber, "A Discussion of Homosexuality," 163-66.

[183]W. Masters and V. Johnson, *Homosexuality in Perspective* (Boston: Little, Brown & Co., 1979).

[184]Socarides, *Homosexuality.*

[185]Regeneration, Inc. of Baltimore, Maryland is one such group. Founded in 1979, it is affiliated with St. Mary's Episcopal Church, Hampden [Editor's note].

[186]E. Pattison and M. Pattison, " 'Ex-gays:' Religiously Mediated Change in Homosexuals," *American Journal of Psychiatry* 137 (1980): 1553-62.

[187]See J.J. Davis, *Evangelical Ethics: Issues Facing the Church Today* (Phillipsburg, N.J.: Presbyterian & Reformed, 1985).

[188]J. Harvey, *The Homosexual Person: New Thinking in Pastoral Care* (Nashville: Abingdon, 1983).

[189]R. Friedman, "The Psychoanalytic Model," 85.

[190]E. Johnson, "Sin, Weakness, and Psychopathology," *Journal of Psychology and Theology* 15 (1987): 218-26.

Chapter Eight

[191]Leviticus 19:2 (*RSV*). See for example, in the New Testament, Matthew 5:16 (*RSV*): "Let your light so shine before men, that they may see your good works and give glory to your Father who is in heaven"; Matt. 5:44 (*RSV*): "But I say to you, Love your enemies and pray for those who persecute you, so that you may be sons of your Father who is in heaven"; Ephesians 5:1-2 (*RSV*): "Therefore be imitators of God, as beloved children. And walk in love, as Christ loved us and gave himself up for us, a fragrant offering and sacrifice to God;" John 14: 21 (*RSV*): "He who has my commandments and

keeps them, he it is who loves me; and he who loves me will be loved by my Father, and I will love him and manifest myself to him;" I John 4:1 (*RSV*): "Beloved, let us love one another; for love is of God, and he who loves is born of God and knows God." Common to these texts is the theme that the Christian moral life is a **witnessing to and sharing in** God's life, being and character. This is the religious meaning for any interpretation of biblical moral teaching on any topic.

[192]In the following discussion, I draw from Philip Turner, *Sex, Money & Power* (Boston: Cowley Publications, 1985), 29-44.

[193]James Nelson, in *Embodiment: An Approach to Sexuality and Christian Theology* (Minnesota: Augsburg, 1978), provides an influential statement of the personalist sex ethic. On page 150, he suggests that Christian ethics may wish to approve of "transmarital relations," i.e. sexual relations between partners married to other persons.

This view is implicit in the Presbyterian General Assembly's Special Committee to Study Human Sexuality Report, which was recommended to the 1991 General Assembly for a two-year study. The report held that the church should not automatically condemn "any sexual relations in which there is genuine equality and mutual respect (p. 40)." Consequently, the report affirms premarital, homosexual, and extramarital sexual relationships marked by equality and respect. Fortunately, these proposals were rejected.

The majority view expressed in the Episcopal Church's Human Affairs Commission Report to the 1991 General Convention shares this view with respect to homosexual relations, recommending the development of liturgies to bless same-sex unions and the ordination of sexually-active homosexual candidates for Holy Orders.

In his book *Living in Sin: A Bishop Looks at His Church*, Episcopal Bishop John Spong advocates sexual same-sex relationships and nonmarital relationships marked by respect and equality. In that book he does not advocate "transmarital" relationships. Another Episcopal proponent of this alternative ethic is The Rev. Raymond J. Lawrence, Jr. in *The Poisoning of Eros: Sexual Values In Conflict* (New York: Augustine Moore Press, 1989). This ethic is also supported by writings of Episcopal seminary professors. See William Countryman's *Dirt, Greed and Sex* and Isabel Carter Heyward's *Touch-*

ing Our Strength: The Erotic as Power and the Love of God (New York: Harper & Row, Publishers, 1989.)

[194]Ruth Tiffany Barnhouse, *Clergy and the Sexual Revolution* (The Alban Institute, 1987). Chapter 1 provides a useful discussion of the sexual revolution.

[195]*Washington Post* (10 March 1991): section A.

[196] Robert Bellah, et al. discuss this individualist morality in *Habits of the Heart: Individualism and Commitment in American Life* (New York: Harper & Row, 1985). Note, however, the critical comments by Jeffrey Stout, *Ethics After Babel* (Boston: Beacon Press, 1988).

Chapter Nine

[197]*The Book of Common Prayer* (English, 1662) (Oxford: Clarendon Press, 1819), 185.

[198]John Shelby Spong, *Living in Sin: A Bishop Rethinks Human Sexuality* (San Francisco: Harper & Row, 1988).

[199]Standing Commission on Human Affairs, "Report of the Commission with Resolutions," *The Blue Book* (New York: Episcopal Church, 1991), 202.

[200]Carter Heyward, *Touching Our Strength: the Erotic as Power and the Love of God* (San Francisco: Harper & Row, 1989), 121.

[201]Ibid, 135-36 [emphasis added].

[202]Ibid, 137.

[203]Ibid., 150.

[204]Robert Williams quoted in Kim Byham, "And the Truth Shall Set You Free: The Rise and Fall of Robert Williams," *The Witness* 73 (April 1990): 12.

Chapter Ten

[205]*New York Times* (3 January 1992).

[206]Stanley Hauerwas, *Community of Character* (Notre Dame: University of Notre Dame Press, 1981), 1.

INDEX